Fuel
FOR SPORT

An introduction to sports nutrition:
what, when, why and how?

Fuel
FOR SPORT

An introduction to sports nutrition:
what, when, why and how?

H. E. Bard

Disclaimer

Whilst every effort has been made to ensure that the contents of this text are true and accurate at the date of going to press, neither the author nor the publisher can accept any legal responsibility for any oversights or omissions, or any injuries or loss sustained as a result of using this material. Before applying any advice from this text, the reader is strongly urged to consult with a suitably qualified physician who can be verified as such. This text is a popular-science styled book written by one person, not an academic text with direct contributions from a wealth of world experts. It should be treated as interesting information only and not as a replacement for expert advice. In short, it is a large report based on a collection of information gained from hundreds of research papers that is offered in one document by a self-taught sports nutritionist.

Send your comments to: steve.caron@dbpublishing.co.uk

Contents

Introduction

As an established science, sports nutrition is arguably not even 30 years old, yet the idea that diets could enhance physical performance has been around since ancient times. It is said that Milo of Croton, a 6th-century BC wrestler from southern Italy, ate 9kg of meat and 9kg of bread, and drank 8.5L of wine, a day. Whether this is true is uncertain, but what is certain is that athletes have been thinking about how best to fuel their activities in order to enhance performance, for thousands of years. If this ancient diet for sport seemed strange, then you may be surprised to learn that the attitude towards large alcohol intakes to aid sporting performance had changed little even by the turn of the 20th century. Marathon runners in the 1908 Olympic Games were believed to have drunk cognac to improve performance, and one athlete was said to have ingested over 20 glasses of beer and half a bottle of wine during his event.

Attitudes towards sports nutrition changed slowly after this, and it was not until the 1970s that research was carried out methodically on trained athletes, especially for hydration and carbohydrate intakes, and that sports nutrition began on its path to becoming a respectable science. This might seem somewhat late, so it is worth pointing out that conventional medicine was not a fully established science until the 1930s. Human nutrition, as we know it today, is still very much in its infancy and many of the claims made for it are still hotly contested. The chemical structures of carbohydrates, fat and proteins were unknown until 1840, and the first vitamins were not discovered until 1913; it was another 20 years or so before indispensible amino acids were identified. So it should come as no surprise that the first books on human nutrition were not available until the 1920s, albeit very different from what we have now; for one thing, the first set of Recommended Daily Allowances (as they were referred to then) were put together by the Food and Nutrition Board (USA) in 1941. Sports nutrition did not really get going or make any great strides until the 1980s, but since then the progress has continued very quickly as funding and interest in the subject grew. To give some idea as to the extent of this, consider the number of 'sports nutrition' papers that were published during each decade since 1960 - the following data was obtained using 'Google scholar' searches (the approximate number of papers is in brackets): 1960-1969 (826); 1970-1979 (2090); 1980-1989 (6540); 1990-

1999 (26,500); 2000-2009 (140,000) and another 25,300 papers in the past two years alone, although it is still only the beginning of August, 2012 at the time of writing.

Human nutrition and sports nutrition

There is a world of difference between human nutrition and sports nutrition, even though (as you might expect) they often overlap. Human nutrition is a much wider subject that is necessarily concerned with the general intakes of all people, from infants to the elderly; the links between diet and diseases, such as heart disease and cancer; the general eating habits of a population; obesity causes and cures, and a host of other issues. Using a similar search method to that above, there were about 129,000 papers published on human nutrition between January 2010 and August 2012, compared with 25,300 papers for sports nutrition in the same period. Even so, this bodes well for sports nutrition, since its aims are far simpler and more focused than human nutrition:

- Sports nutrition refers to dietary consumption that enhances sporting performance and recovery

So it may be argued that owing to sports nutrition's rather narrow focus, its progress has exceeded that of general nutrition because the results are often capable of being more conclusive. For instance, it would be simple to see whether subjects on a sports nutrition trial have increased their muscle mass, but impossible to know with any certainty whether a particular vitamin can help prevent headaches.

About this book

In this book, the term 'average', when used to refer to people, usually means 'normal/healthy' as defined by the body mass index (BMI) *(see 4.2)*, but this measure might not include some athletes because many have an above-average body mass (according to their BMI) owing to their greater muscle accumulation. However, this should not be exaggerated, since most people who exercise regularly still fit within the compounds of BMI measures - only very dedicated athletes will deviate from it. If the term 'average' is meant in the mathematical sense, this will be clear from the context.

There are many formulae in this book, some of which are necessary for individual requirements, and some merely for experimental purposes or for clarification of understanding. So even though it is useful and interesting for some to know all such formulae, it is tedious and unnecessary for many others. For this reason, all the calculations required for personal requirements, and many experimental ones, can easily be obtained via the corresponding Excel program. Look for the calculator symbol:

This symbol will be found next to any calculation that corresponds to an Excel program. In many cases the symbol will be to the right of a sub-heading; this indicates that all calculations within that section have a corresponding Excel program. It is also worth noting that two useful Excel workbooks are included that are not mentioned in the body of this text; *Conversions* and *Personal data sheet*. All measurements in this book follow the metric system, so the *Conversions* sheet will be very useful for those who are more familiar with the imperial system. The *Personal data sheet* is a printable sheet that may be used by athletes to record all their specific intakes and other important details according to their training programme. The Excel files can be downloaded free of charge, see **Excel download and programs** on page 329 for the link. Please note that there are several macros included in the sheets, so you may have to enable them before use. If they are not enabled all features should still work, except, of course, the macro buttons.

Some sections might be particularly difficult to understand, or not strictly necessary for understanding this text, such as the theoretical calculations of the number of fat cells (**Chapter 5**). Such sections will be marked with the exclamation symbol:

This symbol will appear to the left of any sub-heading in a section that may be skipped.

There are many terms and sentences that are highlighted in boldface or bullet-pointed to enable the reader to find them more easily. Such terms and sentences might be interesting or important advice, or include a list of information related to a heading or sub-heading that might be hard to locate if immersed in the body of the text:

- Important phrases are highlighted in bold and/or bullet-pointed.

Everyone's an amateur sports nutritionist

You may have heard it said that 'everyone is an amateur psychologist', but these days it seems that 'everyone is an amateur nutritionist or sports nutritionist'. There is seemingly endless advice coming from family and friends, daytime television, glossy magazines, newspapers, websites and books written by so-called experts. Yet such advice is often misleading, misinformed, vague, or entirely unfounded. So one of the aims of this book is to address many of the misconceptions that refuse to go away, which is why there are so many detailed examples of what *not* to do, or of what is *untrue*. Sometimes, the theory behind the misconception is so strong that it is first necessary to disabuse people of the wrong idea before explaining the right one. Without doing so, questions based on the misconceptions may continue to be raised.

Many of those reading this book, especially those new to sports nutrition, may expect definitive answers for all their wants, but science does not work that way and the complexity of the human mind and body makes this all the more difficult. This book aims to report the available information 'as it is', which may mean that in many cases the information will be vague or contrary to what you might have hoped for, but better this than to be misled or misinformed. Things must be kept in perspective, anything else would be dishonest, deceptive and perhaps even dangerous. That said, do not take this to mean that all is bad news, it is not; indeed, most is very good news because knowledge and application of sports nutrition will almost certainly produce significant results.

In some cases things are quite well established, such as the recommended timing and amount of carbohydrate post-exercise, but this does not mean that these will not be improved upon in the future; in fact, there is currently much research on the benefits of the different types of carbohydrates, and each may have its own benefits and unique timings. In other cases the advice has changed significantly: not so long ago you might well have been advised to ingest 125-350ml of water every 10-20 minutes during a marathon; the advice is very different now, even though many websites (and even books) still promote this erroneous, and potentially very dangerous, recommendation.

Recommended reading

At the back of this text there is a list of 'recommended reading' that corresponds to each chapter, and most also include sub-headings to make it easier to find the required information. However, the recommended reading does not adhere to any typical or conventional guide, such as the Oxford referencing system or the Harvard referencing system. The entries in the recommended reading list are in the order: Internet link and date (in brackets) on which the paper was accepted, full title of the paper in bold, then a selected cut-and-pasted portion from the paper; for example:

http://sph.sagepub.com/content/4/2/142.short (2012)

Emerging Supplements in Sports

An Internet search of common fitness and bodybuilding sites and of the most commonly identified supplements, including glutamine, choline, methoxyisoflavone, quercetin, zinc/magnesium aspartate, and nitric oxide… Scientific evidence is not available to support the use of these supplements for performance enhancement.

However, some papers include a personal note; these are introduced as 'My note' and written in italics:

http://www.ncbi.nlm.nih.gov/pmc/articles/PMC3070624/?tool=pubmd (2011)

International Society of Sports Nutrition position stand: meal frequency

My note: A comprehensive and easy-to-read report about meal frequency, including 88 references.

There are also the odd few papers that include a cut-and-pasted portion as well as a 'My note' entry, and even fewer include only the Internet link, date, and title.

The aim of the cut-and-pasted portion (or 'My note') is to whet the appetite of the reader, so we hope that the system used for the recommended reading will actually encourage you to check the information in this book; we do not believe that the conventional systems actively invite non-academic readers to do this. The short extracts below each paper's title should make it easier for you to choose which might be of interest to you, but nevertheless, we urge that after completing a chapter you immediately go to the recommended reading list for that chapter and read the titles and their corresponding extracts as if they were an extension of the chapter. As you do so it would be a good idea to make a note of any that you find particularly interesting so that you can check these papers at your earliest convenience. The papers are very easy to find as each is provided with a direct link, and even if a problem occurs with the link, they can easily be retrieved: all papers were obtained using Google scholar or PubMed - simply enter the full title into one of these (we recommend trying PubMed first) and there should be no problem retrieving the desired paper (*see **Useful websites for sports nutrition**, page 326*).

A conscious effort was made to include as many recent papers - most are less than 10 years old, and many are less than two or three years old - and from a wide range of countries. There are many full papers or articles, or at least informative abstracts that include the aims, method, results and conclusions, some opposing papers (to add balance), and several that are not directly related to what is in the text, but were thought particularly interesting. There are over 360 links to carefully chosen papers, and all of these lead to more direct links to similar papers.

There are no direct 'references' in the body of this text, and there are two main reasons for this. The first is that constant citations immediately after each idea or piece of information cause an interruption to the reading flow, which may hinder understanding and may cause the text to appear untidy. That apart, the second reason for no references is far more important. Consider the following:

Chocolate milk is an effective drink to aid recovery after endurance exercise (Thomas et al., 2009); perhaps welcomed news by chocolate lovers who also like their sports.

The statement before the citation is true, and the citation genuine, yet it can easily be taken out of context. The paper included only nine subjects, all of whom were male, and all of whom were trained cyclists. Without just these three pieces of extra information, many might make unfounded assumptions about chocolate milk as a post-exercise recovery drink. Does chocolate milk work just as well on female cyclists? What about other endurance athletes, male or female? How about non-trained cyclists or other non-trained athletes? Can we infer that chocolate milk is better than milk and honey or milk and sugar? The list goes on. We are not criticising the authors, and perhaps chocolate milk does indeed benefit trained and non-trained athletes, male and female, endurance athletes of all kinds etcetera, but it would be careless to come to such conclusions based on just one small study. So, such citations are not present in this text as we believe them to be misleading, and in some cases, entirely misplaced. In our experience, websites are often the most guilty of misplaced (an understatement) references; some cite medical papers that have no relation to sport *or* nutrition, let alone 'sports nutrition' itself. It is often part of medical trials to monitor the strength or oxygen capacity of subjects, but the reasons for doing so are completely unrelated to sport. In any case, such trials may include only a small number of subjects of a narrow age range, from a particular culture, with a high BMI, and all with a particular disease; hardy a representation of the masses. Yet even papers that represent such a constricted group of people (on a non-sport-related trial) will be cited by some websites. Still, if a citation is grossly misleading or misplaced it seems that there is little that can be done about it (newspapers do it all the time) - at least not in the UK. As things are, health/ sports shops and websites can get away with their carefully worded claims even if they are only remotely related to the paper to which they refer, and such shaky evidence is very much part of the reason that so many supplements have wild 'scientific' claims made for them *(see **Chapter 8**)*.

While this book does include some advice about food and diet, there are no recipes as it seems pointless to offer only a handful of recipes since there are so many individuals to consider. In some sports nutrition books, recipes make up a large percentage - often as much as a quarter - yet may still fail to cater for a large number of people, hence why this was not considered either. In any case, the term *sports nutrition* is not synonymous with *cookcry for athletes* (another book perhaps?). Nonetheless, the Australian Institute of Sport provides an excellent selection of recipes for sportspeople. Each dish is provided with the main nutritional information per serving, and there is even a wide selection of recipes from around the world *(see **Useful websites for sports nutrition**, page 326)*.

Physicians and nutritionists

Throughout this book you will notice the reader is often advised to see a medical doctor, dietitian or sport physician, but not a nutritionist or sports nutritionist. The reason is that nutritionist, nutritional therapist, sports nutritionist, and similar, are not protected terms in many countries, including the UK, parts of Canada, most US states and Australia. This means that anyone can set themselves up as a sports nutritionist or human nutritionist with few, if any, qualifications. Many do take relevant courses, but these are often short correspondence (so-called) diplomas from a self-governing body; they are unaccountable, unrecognised and perhaps only registered by those issuing the diploma. This is not to suggest that all those calling themselves nutritionists or sports nutritionists are poorly versed in their respective subjects; no doubt, many have years of training and practical experience and are very competent in their field. Furthermore, there are many well-regarded universities that offer undergraduate and postgraduate degrees in nutrition and related subjects, and these *are* recognised by creditable organisations. As just one example, the Nutrition Society in the UK confers the title Associate Nutritionist (A Nutr) and Associate Public Health Nutritionist (APH Nutr) only to those who provide evidence of a suitable bachelor's degree. Applicants who wish to be conferred the titles Registered Nutritionist (R Nutr) or Registered Public Health Nutritionist (RPH Nutr) must further provide evidence of at least three years' hands-on experience, and be able to demonstrate their ability to work safely and effectively and agree to abide by a code of ethics. It is unfortunate that such people might be sharing similar titles with those who bought their diploma, bachelor's, master's, or even doctorate, on the Internet.

On the other hand, medical doctor, dietitian, nurse and dentist are all examples of protected terms, and it is illegal for anyone in the UK, parts of Europe and much of North America to refer to themselves as such unless they hold recognised qualifications and are registered to do so.

In the UK, Sport and Exercise Medicine only became a recognised speciality by the General Medical Council in 2005. The training is long and rigorous, and those interested first need to go through medical school, then complete a five-year specialist programme before being entered in the specialist register - there are several speciality paths available. The continual training of these sports physicians is compulsory, as in all medical fields, and their all-round knowledge of both exercise and medicine, as well as the long, varied and compulsory practical experience makes them arguably the highest-qualified of all those that work in sport and exercise medicine. As it is, the term 'sport(s) physician' is not a protected term, but in this text the term is used to refer to a recognised and registered medical doctor that has further qualifications in sports and exercise medicine; the same as, or equivalent to, those described above.

Do not be swayed by post nominal letters (PhD, Dip Nutr, etc.), elaborate certificates, national awards, number of books written (or sold), famous persons treated, TV and Radio spots, newspaper columns, or where or how many lectures have been given. Many of the least qualified and most guilty of offering misplaced and uninformed advice could tick off each of these and more. In short, *prefer real medicine to magic potions, and hard evidence to soft notions.*

1 HUMAN ENERGY

Energy is the ability or capacity to do work. People require energy to function: move, breath, digest, keep warm, keep cool, sleep and so on. Most of what we eat is an energy source that is transformed into available energy; it is sometimes used quickly or else stored for future use. This chapter introduces the main aspects of human energy and related issues, including energy systems of the body, muscle fibres, exercise intensity and fatigue.

1.1 Energy sources

There are four sources of human energy: carbohydrates, protein, fat and alcohol, and all except alcohol are essential for health and well-being, and as fuel for activity. Each provides a certain amount of food energy, often measured in calories, that is used to a greater or lesser degree depending on the type of activity, intensity, duration and several other factors. It is common for the energy of specific foods and the energy needs of humans to be described in terms of calories, though in many cases it should in fact be **kilocalories (kcal)**. For example, we are often told that the average woman needs 2000 'calories' a day, but this should be 2000kcal (i.e., 2,000,000 calories). Some texts avoid the use of 'kcal' or 'kilocalories' because they are considered a little clumsy to keep saying and/or the general public may not recognise the terms. To get past this, many use Calorie (notice the capital 'c') in written texts, and the abbreviation 'Cal' rather than 'cal'. In this text 'kcal' is used throughout, though the term 'calorie' will be used when referring to them in general.

A calorie is the amount of energy required to increase the temperature of one gramme of water by one degree Celsius at standard atmospheric pressure. However, some countries use the joule, which is the International System of Units (SI units) standard measure of energy. One calorie is approximately equivalent to 4.2 joules (J), but similarly for calories, joules are normally referred to as kilojoules (kJ) when describing food energy and human energy matters.

Each of the essential energy sources - carbohydrates, protein and fat - are described in subsequent chapters; for the mean time, their fundamental uses and approximate energy values are given below:

- **carbohydrate** is mainly a short-term energy supply: **1g ≈ 4kcal**
- **protein** is mainly an emergency energy supply: **1g ≈ 4kcal**
- **fat** is mainly a long-term energy supply: **1g ≈ 9kcal**
- **alcohol** is a short-term energy supply: **1g ≈ 7kcal**

1.1.1 Alcohol storage and effects

Each of the macronutrients (carbohydrates, protein and fat) are stored and used in different ways; these are described in chapters 2, 3 and 4, respectively, so this sub-section describes only the storage and effects of alcohol.

Alcohol

Carbohydrates, protein and fat can all be transported to, and broken down in, muscle cells. Alcohol, on the other hand, cannot be used directly by muscles for energy during exercise; only the liver can break down alcohol. Alcohol is first absorbed into the body through the stomach and small intestine; food will slow down this absorption, and that is why its effects are far quicker if drunk on an empty stomach. It is then distributed throughout the body via the bloodstream, reaching the heart, brain, muscles and other tissues within just a few minutes. The body cannot store alcohol as it can the other energy sources, so it must get rid of it. The liver first converts it into a toxic substance, then into a non-toxic substance, and finally into carbon dioxide and water. The carbon dioxide and water are excreted by the body via urine, breathing and perspiration.

The exercising muscle cannot use alcohol as an energy source - in fact, it reduces the body's ability to produce usable blood sugar, and so you end up with less energy and less endurance capacity. Exercising faster or harder will not affect the alcohol breakdown speed either, because the liver works at a fixed pace. Cramps are also associated with alcohol and exercise, and studies have shown that after either chronic alcohol ingestion or acute alcohol intoxication, protein synthesis is depressed.

Drinking alcohol 24 hours before exercise will greatly increase the risk of muscle cramp. Alcohol also affects the speed at which certain injuries will heal because it increases the bleeding and swelling around the soft tissue injuries - sprains, bruises and cuts - so you take longer to heal. There is plenty of evidence that shows that alcohol adversely alters the immune system, and there is recent experimental evidence that suggests that alcohol ingested after exercise may change the viscosity of the blood. Moreover, there is increasing evidence that suggests that chronic alcohol ingestion adversely effects the brain, liver and cardiovascular system.

1.1.2 Energy systems

Adenosine triphosphate (ATP) is a multifunctional molecule and is the energy source of every cell in the body. ATP consists of three phosphates (hence *tri*phosphate) but when a cell requires energy one phosphate is released and ATP becomes **adenosine diphosphate (ADP)**, as now there are only two phosphates. In some instances a second phosphate is released forming **adenosine monophosphate (AMP)**, as now there is only one phosphate remaining. At rest muscles have only a very small amount of ATP, enough to last about three seconds or only one second at maximum intensity. To continue exercising, ATP must be regenerated from one of the three energy systems.

1) ATP-PC system (ATP phosphocreatine)

ATP-PC, also called the **phosphagen system**, is stored in the muscles. It generates maximum bursts of energy for speed and strength activities that last up to about six seconds; short sprints, near-maximum dead lifts, fast and powerful punching permutations, and so on. This is why full speed and power cannot be continued for more than a few seconds.

Phosphocreatine (PC) regenerates ATP quickly. PC breaks down into creatine and phosphate and the free phosphate then bonds to an ADP molecule; thus forming a new ATP molecule ready to be used again for energy. The ATP-PC system releases energy very quickly but is also very limited and offers only three to four kcal of energy. If exercise is to be continued, ATP must come from other fuels, such as glycogen or fat, so other energy systems must take over *(see 2. and 3., below)*.

Creatine

Creatine is a compound made naturally in the body to supply energy; the muscles make about 2-3g of creatine a day. It is produced mainly in the liver from three amino acids: glycine, arginine, and methionine. It is then transported from the liver via the blood to the muscle cells where it is combined to phosphates to make phosphocreatine. Once PC is broken down into ATP energy it can be recycled into PC again, or converted into another substance called creatinine, which is removed via the kidneys in the urine.

Creatine comes from fish and meat only, thus vegetarians have no dietary sources. Large doses of creatine are required to enhance performance, far more than is reasonable to obtain from your diet. For instance, you would require about 2kg of raw steak a day to load the muscles with creatine. The average person stores about 120g of creatine, mainly in the skeletal muscles, and of this 60 to 70 per cent (72-84 g) is stored as PC and 30 to 40 per cent (36-48 g) as free creatine. Supplementation with creatine is very common amongst athletes *(see **Chapter 8** for more on **creatine**).*

2) Anaerobic glycolytic system

This system, also called the **Lactic acid system**, produces ATP to last up to about 90 seconds. This system does not use oxygen, indeed anaerobic means *without oxygen.* The anaerobic glycolytic system uses complex carbohydrates in the form of muscle **glycogen** (a chain of glucose molecules), which is broken down into glucose for use as energy. In the absence of oxygen the glucose breaks down quickly to form ATP and lactic acid. Each glucose molecule produces only two ATP molecules during anaerobic exercise, thus the body's glycogen stores dwindle quickly and a third, more efficient, system will be required if exercise is to continue *(see **item 3**, below).*

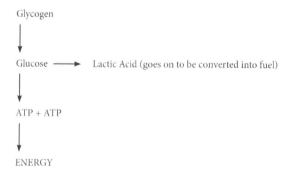

Glycogen

Glucose ⟶ Lactic Acid (goes on to be converted into fuel)

ATP + ATP

ENERGY

Lactic acid

When exercise intensity is reduced or stopped lactic acid has two fates.

- Some is converted into another substance which is then broken down into ATP, therefore a valuable fuel for aerobic exercise.
- The rest is carried from the muscles to the liver via the bloodstream. Here it is converted back into glucose and released back into the bloodstream for energy, or stored as glycogen in the liver, where the cycle repeats.

Lactic acid is normally cleared within 90 seconds of exercise, so contrary to popular belief, muscle soreness and stiffness after hard training is not owing to the lactic acid build up. It is a build-up of hydrogen ions and acidity that causes the burning feeling during or immediately after exercise; however, lactic acid does eventually cause fatigue and prevent further muscle contractions.

3) Aerobic system

The aerobic system generates ATP from the breakdown of carbohydrates (**glycolysis**) and fat (**lipolysis**), both in the presence of oxygen. This system is not nearly as fast as the other two systems, but has the distinct advantage of producing much larger amounts of ATP molecules. Aerobic fitness can boost the body's recovery from **high intensity intermittent training (HIIT)** *(see 5.1.1)*, partly because it improves lactate removal and phosphocreatine restoration. All physical activity begins with the ATP-PC and anaerobic systems, but after a few minutes the body switches to the aerobic system.

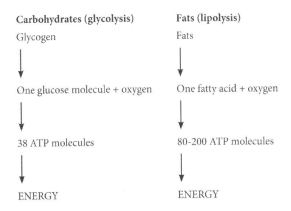

Carbohydrates (glycolysis)

Glycogen

↓

One glucose molecule + oxygen

↓

38 ATP molecules

↓

ENERGY

Fats (lipolysis)

Fats

↓

One fatty acid + oxygen

↓

80-200 ATP molecules

↓

ENERGY

Most carbohydrate, the fuel for glycolysis, comes from muscle glycogen. Further required glucose will come from the bloodstream as the need becomes more important, usually as exercise continues for longer than one hour, as this is when muscle glycogen dwindles. After about two hours of training (at > 70% VO_2 max - *see below*), almost all muscle glycogen is depleted. Muscles are then primarily fuelled by glucose from the bloodstream and also gradually more and more from fat (**lipolytic glycolysis**). Glucose from the bloodstream is from the breakdown of liver glycogen or carbohydrates consumed 'during' exercise.

Overall, the energy demands from aerobic exercise is lower and slower, so there is time for oxygen to be included in the process. This leads to one glucose molecule creating up to 38 ATP molecules, and one fatty acid molecule producing 80 to 200 ATP molecules, depending on the type of fatty acid.

VO_2 max

The volume of oxygen you can consume while exercising at your maximum capacity can be used to measure fitness levels. VO_2 max is the maximum amount of oxygen (in millilitres (ml)) you can use in one minute per kg of body mass and is widely accepted as the best measure of cardiovascular fitness levels, but it is limited by an individual's ability to deliver oxygen to the exercising muscles; we are not all the same. Untrained but otherwise healthy males may have a VO_2 max of about 40ml per kg of body mass per minute; females are slightly lower at about 30ml per kg of body mass per minute. The fitter you are the higher your VO_2 max, and consequently your fitness levels, will be. However, your VO_2 max is largely determined genetically so being able to increase it significantly is further limited by many other factors including, age, gender and current fitness levels. For some individuals, training may as much as double their VO_2 max, yet for others the improvement will be marginal. Those that excel in endurance sports, such as rowers, cyclists and skiers, tend to have a very high VO_2 max; male endurance athletes commonly have a VO_2 max into the 80s, and female athletes into the 70s.

There are self-test methods, some of which are more accurate than others, but if you are serious about your training, it is safer and more accurate to have your VO_2 max tested professionally.

1.1.3 Muscle fibres

Skeletal muscles can be broken down into two broad types; slow twitch (type I) and fast twitch (type II):

- **Slow twitch (ST)** muscles use all three energy systems but mainly the aerobic system, have a high resistance to fatigue and are better equipped for aerobic exercise.
- **Fast twitch (FT)** muscles also use all three energy systems, but mainly the ATP-PC and anaerobic systems, and are thus more suited for bursts of speed and power but are quicker to fatigue than slow twitch muscle fibres.

Slow twitch muscle fibres are so called because they have a slow contraction time; they have a low power output but can be used for hours, which is why they are more suitable for endurance activities.

Fast twitch muscle fibres come in three distinct fibre types: type IIa, type IIx and type IIb. Type IIa have a moderately fast contraction time, a medium power output and a fairly high resistance to fatigue; all relative to the other fibre types. These fibre types are used for long-term anaerobic activity of less than 30 minutes. Type IIx have a fast contraction time and a high power output, with an average resistance to fatigue; suitable for anaerobic activity of less than five minutes. Type IIb have the fastest contraction time and the highest power output, but the lowest resistance to fatigue; suitable for very short-term anaerobic activity of less than one minute.

Many people fight a losing battle by trying to excel in sports for which they are naturally unsuited. We are all born with specific amounts of FT and ST fibres; the ratio is determined before birth, and the proportions vary considerably among individuals. This is why we are more suited to certain sports; power-sport people, sprinters for example, have more FT fibres, whereas distance runners have more ST fibres.

It is common to read that type IIb muscle fibres have the largest cross-sectional area of all muscle fibres, but research into adolescent, non-trained men and women shows otherwise. Among men, the type IIa muscle fibres are significantly larger than other types, and for women type I, or both type I and IIa, are normally largest. The muscle-fibre distribution between men and women are not significantly different, but the cross-sectional area of all muscle types is larger in men than in women. As we age, our muscle fibres, mainly type II, decrease in size and number, and are replaced with fat and connective tissue, but good and continual training can greatly reduce and slow down these effects.

1.2 Energy in use

Carbohydrate, fat and protein are all used to supply us with energy, but the proportions vary greatly depending on:

- intensity
- duration
- fitness level
- pre-exercise diet

1.2.1 Exercise intensity

The **heart rate (HR)** is a measure of **heart beats per minute (bpm)**, and the **maximum heart rate (MHR)** is given by: **MHR = 220 - (age in years) bpm**

Exercise intensity - also called, training intensity - is often unwisely given as a direct correspondence to a percentage of the maximum heart rate. For instance, medium intensity is given as 80 to 85 per cent of a person's MHR, so since a 30-year-old person has an MHR of 190 bpm, this means he will have to exercise at a heart rate of 152-162 bpm to attain medium intensity. However, a simple subtraction does not take into consideration a person's age, gender, fitness level and so on. The term *medium intensity* may sound harmless enough, but it might be dangerously high for one 30-year-old and futilely low for another. A far better way to consider exercise intensity is with respect to your VO_2 max.

- **low intensity** (<50% of your VO_2 max) is fuelled mainly by fat.
- **medium intensity** (50-70% of your VO_2 max) uses similar amounts of each of muscle glycogen and fat.
- **high intensity** (>70% of your VO_2 max) is fuelled mainly by muscle glycogen.

Figure 1.1 below shows that the higher the intensity, the more muscle glycogen is used for fuel over fat. Conversely, the lower the intensity, the more fat is used for fuel over muscle glycogen. However, do not let this mislead you to think that low intensity exercise necessarily burns more fat.

Example 1.2.1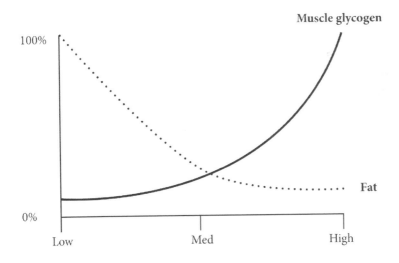

Consider a person who weighs 60kg. Now consider her kcal burned during a low intensity exercise when compared to those burned during a medium intensity exercise. Let us assume that this person walking at 5 kph (low intensity) burns a typical 200kcal an hour, where a 'generous' 95 per cent of the fuel comes from fat, and jogging at about 12 kph burns a typical 800kcal an hour, where only 60 per cent of the fuel comes from fat. After walking for one hour she will have burned 190kcal from fat, yet if she jogged for half that time she would have burned 240kcal from fat. In terms of weight, she will have burned about 21g of fat from walking for one hour compared with about 27g of fat from jogging for just 30 minutes.

Fig 1.1 Fuel Mixture/Exercise Intensity

The previous example leads to another equally important consideration, **exercise duration**. Muscle glucose is quite limited, and as you continue exercising muscle glycogen decreases and energy from blood glucose increases *(see **Figure 1.2** below)*. Some important things worth noting about energy reduction are:

- Fat used for energy increases as exercise is prolonged, but it cannot be burned without carbohydrates present.
- On average a person has enough muscle glycogen to fuel 90 to 180 minutes of endurance exercise.
- Higher intensity exercise means faster depletion of muscle glycogen.
- During interval training - i.e. a mix of aerobic and anaerobic training, muscle glycogen stores deplete after 45 to 90 minutes.
- During mainly anaerobic exercises, muscle glycogen stores deplete within 30 to 45 minutes.
- Once muscle glycogen stores are depleted, protein makes an increasing energy contribution.

Fig 1.2 Fuel mixture/Exercice duration

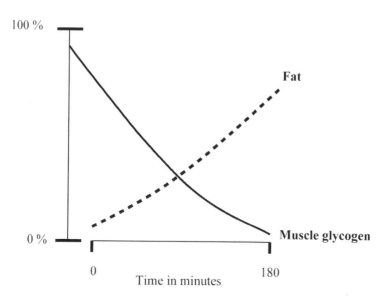

Trained versus untrained persons

An increased training ability means a greater capacity to burn fatty acids in each muscle cell; fat will break down more quickly at any given intensity in a trained person, which in turn allows for a greater sparing of valuable glycogen. This is very important, since glycogen is in much shorter supply than fat. Hence, a trained person will be able to exercise for longer before muscle glycogen is depleted and fatigue sets in. *Figure 1.3* shows a vague idea of the differences between trained and untrained persons, so it should be treated as a simple and limited visual aid only.

Fig 1.3 Fat and glycogen usage (trained v untrained)

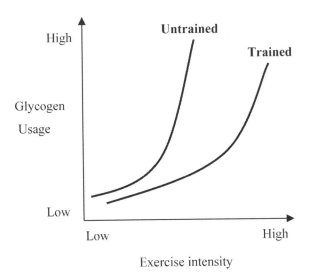

1.2.2 Energy systems as used

Virtually all activities use all three systems to some extent. No single energy system is used exclusively and at any given time energy is being derived from each of the three systems *(see Figure 1.4 below)*. **In every activity ATP is always used and replaced by PC.**

Fig 1.4 Percentage usage of energy systems

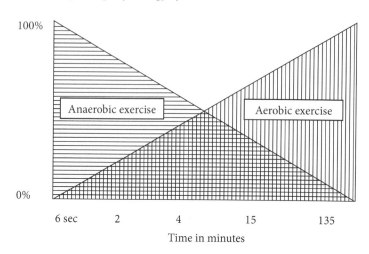

For explosive activities lasting up to about five or six seconds, such as a sprint start or a short power-punch permutation, the existing store of ATP is the primary energy source. For high-power and high-speed activities of about six to 30 seconds, such as 100m to 200m sprints, ATP-PC is the primary energy source, along with some muscle glycogen broken down through the anaerobic glycolysis energy system.

During power endurance activities, such as 400m to 800m athletics or a few high-intensity boxing rounds, muscle glycogen is the main energy source, where ATP is produced via both the anaerobic glycolytic and aerobic systems. In aerobic power activities, such as 5-10km runs or many rounds of boxing, muscle glycogen is the primary energy source producing ATP via aerobic glycolysis. During aerobic endurance activities lasting two or more hours - half or full marathons, for instance - muscle glycogen, intra-muscular fat, and fat from adipose tissue are the main fuels used.

Fig 1.5 Summary of energy systems used for different exercise types

Exercise type	Main energy system(s)	Main storage fuels used
Maximal short burst (< 6 sec)	ATP-PC (phosphagen)	ATP and PC
High intensity (6-30 sec)	ATP-PC Anaerobic glycolytic	ATP and PC Muscle glycogen

High intensity (0.5 -15 min)	Anaerobic glycolytic Aerobic	Muscle glycogen
Mod-high intensity (15-60 min)	Aerobic	Muscle glycogen and adipose tissue
Mod-high intensity (60-90 min)	Aerobic	Muscle glycogen, liver glycogen, blood glucose, intra-muscular fat and adipose tissue
Moderate intensity (90+ min)	Aerobic	Muscle glycogen, liver glycogen, blood glucose, intra-muscular fat and adipose tissue

1.2.3 The start of exercise

Initially a build up of lactic acid takes place because the heart and lungs will not have caught up with the sudden energy demands. However, gentle exercise means that oxygen can keep pace with these demands and so the initial accumulation of lactic acid is easily removed; hence the benefits of easing into your training. For the first 15 minutes of exercise (depending on fitness levels), the main form of fuel is carbohydrate. This is followed by less carbohydrate and more fat *(see **Figure 1.5** above)*. If you begin intensely, lactic acid will build up in the muscles without getting the chance to be removed on time. Furthermore, oxygen will not keep pace with the energy demands, and fatigue will quickly result, so you will have to slow down or stop altogether. Keep in mind that **if you start fast or intensely, you will finish early.**

A gentle warm up gets the heart and lungs working, and as a result oxygen delivered to the muscles increases. Always start exercising slowly or moderately, and only when adequately warmed up should you build up to optimal speed or power. This will prevent a large **oxygen debt** *(see below)*, and help prevent an early depletion of glycogen.

Even when you have reached the point where the aerobic system is your main energy supply, the anaerobic system will still cut back in. It is comparable to switching gears in a car, depending on what the situation demands. For instance, if you want to run uphill at the same pace as on the flat, your body will need to switch systems. This switching back to the anaerobic system only occurs for a short time because of the lactic acid build-up, but it can be easily and quickly removed aerobically afterwards - by running back down the hill, for example. In fact, if you train for long enough, the body will switch gears for a short time anyway.

This changing of energy systems is one of the primary reasons for that uneasy feeling of fatigue experienced during training. When it happens and for how long depends on each person, though it will take longer to occur and last for less time as your fitness level increases. This same principle of switching from aerobic to anaerobic systems (and vice versa) applies to interval training - i.e., training at various speeds and power levels such as that in football or boxing. In these cases the lactic acid accumulates and is then removed during the interval - at half time or between rounds, for example.

Oxygen debt

This occurs when the demand for oxygen is greater than the actual supply. Hence, the athlete is working hard and breathing in a lot of oxygen, but cannot absorb enough to cope with the level of activity. When this happens, the body is mainly using the anaerobic system, and as a result there is a build up of lactic acid. This system can only be sustained for about 90 seconds before fatigue sets in and recovery time is necessary. The amount of oxygen owed to the body in order to recover is called the **oxygen debt**. If, for example, you sprint 400m you will mainly be using the anaerobic system from start to finish. When you have finished the race you will breathe vigorously for some moments. This additional oxygen that must be taken into the body after vigorous exercise to restore all systems to their normal states is the oxygen debt being paid.

1.3 Fatigue

In everyday language, 'fatigue' normally refers to either mental fatigue or physical fatigue; general feelings of lethargy or tiredness, or simply a general decrease in concentration. In terms of exercise, though, fatigue refers to a training-induced burning sensation within the exercising muscles, and is therefore often called muscle fatigue. It is an inability to sustain a certain power output or speed; a mismatch between energy demand by muscles, and energy supply, has occurred. It happens in all sports: when a footballer is simply unable to sprint for a ball, when a lifter cannot lift the weight, when a fighter cannot throw an effective punch, and so on. The athlete is generally slower or utterly unable to perform the task in hand. However, fatigue is more than just a physical reaction - in fact, it is now considered to be primarily an emotion; a complex reaction that aims to protect the body from damage.

1.3.1 Fatigue during anaerobic exercise

When the demand for ATP exceeds the readily available supply for explosive activities (normally less than 30 second's duration) such as power punches, sprints and heavy lifts of maximal output, fatigue sets in. For exercises between 30 seconds and 30 minutes, fatigue is caused by a different mechanism. Lactic acid removed from the blood stream cannot keep pace with the rate of lactic acid production, so a gradual build up of muscle acidity occurs and thus reduces its ability to maintain intense contractions. Too much acid in muscles will inhibit further contractions and will cause cell death. The burning feeling is a warning that the exercising muscle has too high a concentration of acid. The burn makes you stop (at least it should) which will prevent the cell from being damaged; the best solution is to reduce the intensity before the burning stage occurs, if possible. This will lower the lactic acid production and consequently its build-up; it will also allow the muscles to switch to the aerobic system and therefore allow you to continue exercising. In a short time you will be able to switch back to the anaerobic system again, and as a result increase the intensity once more.

1.3.2 Fatigue during aerobic exercise

Fatigue occurs during moderate to high intensity (i.e., > 50% VO_2 max) exercises that last longer than one hour owing to depletion of muscle glycogen stores. The liver can help maintain blood sugar levels and offer a supply of carbohydrate to the exercising muscles; however, stores are very limited. Eventually fatigue occurs as a result of both muscle and liver glycogen depletion and **hypoglycaemia** (deficiency of glucose in the blood stream).

Fatigue that occurs during low-to-moderate intensity exercise that lasts more than three hours is caused by additional factors. When glycogen stores are exhausted, the body switches to the aerobic lipolytic system, and fat is able to supply most of the fuel required for low-intensity exercise. However, even though we have comparatively high fat reserves, fat alone cannot be converted into energy fast enough to supply the demand of the exercising muscles. Even slowing right down will eventually make no difference, as other factors will cause fatigue, such as a rise in concentration levels of **serotonin**, a neurotransmitter in the brain that is associated with mental fatigue. As the levels of serotonin increase, so do the levels of tryptophan (an amino acid), which indirectly causes the production of more serotonin; a vicious cycle begins.

During prolonged exercise, as liver glycogen is depleted, working muscles release increasing amounts of amino acids. This has a reverse effect, as by doing so the muscle will become weaker, not stronger as desired.

1.3.3 Delaying fatigue

Glycogen is used in virtually every type of activity, so glycogen stores in muscles - and in certain events, your liver - before exercise will directly affect your performance. Loosely speaking, the greater the pre-exercise glycogen stores, the longer you will be able to maintain exercise intensity, and the longer you will be able to delay fatigue. You can also delay fatigue by reducing the rate you use up muscle glycogen; this is achieved by gradually building up to your optimal intensity. In short, *pace yourself!*

2 CARBOHYDRATES (CH_2O)

Carbohydrates are a group of organic compounds, including sugars, starches and fibre. Chemically, they are a bonding of carbon, hydrogen and oxygen of varying ratios, depending on the type, and are thus often simplified to just CH_2O or even just CHO. Carbohydrates are the main energy source and the most readily available in the body. This chapter discusses the various types of carbohydrates and the finely-tuned intakes that vary according to the activity concerned and the body mass of the athlete. The glycaemic index and the much-neglected glycaemic load are also described.

2.1 Carbohydrate storage

Carbohydrates are stored as glycogen in the muscles and in the liver, along with three-to-four parts of water. This is why a low-carbohydrates means loss of glycogen stores, and therefore a loss of mainly water, *not* fat. For an average person, about 300-400g of glycogen is stored in the muscles, and about 60-100g in the liver. Liver glycogen is for maintenance of blood glucose levels at rest and during prolonged exercise.

2.2 Types of carbohydrate

Carbohydrates are traditionally classified according to their chemical structure: simple carbohydrates (sugars) and complex carbohydrates (starches and fibres). These terms simply refer to the number of sugar units in the molecule.

Simple carbohydrates have very small molecules containing only one (monosaccharaides) or two (disaccharides) sugar units, some examples are given below.
Monosaccharaides (1-sugar unit) include:

1. glucose (dextrose)
2. fructose (fruit sugar)
3. galactose (less sweet than glucose, often found in dairy products)
4. xylose (wood sugar, found the embryos of most edible plants)

Disaccharides (2-sugar units) include:

1. sucrose (table sugar, a joined glucose and fructose molecule)
2. lactose (milk sugar, a joined glucose and galactose molecule)
3. maltose (malt sugar, two joined glucose molecules)

Disaccharides are broken down into monosaccharaides before being absorbed into the bloodstream.

Complex carbohydrates (**polysaccharides**) consist of a larger number of sugar units (mostly glucose) joined together, anything from three and upwards, often up to several 1000. The general formula is given as $(CH_2O)_n$, where n is three or greater. However, it should be noted that not all carbohydrates conform to this and not all that do are necessarily carbohydrates. Complex carbohydrates include:

1. **starch**, which has two polysaccharide components, amylose and amylopectin
2. **non-starch polysaccharides** (dietary/insoluble fibre): such as cellulose and pectin

There are five main types of polysaccharide.

- **Starch** includes foods such as cereals, grains and some root vegetables, such as potatoes and parsnips.
- **Dextrin** is formed when foods containing starch (e.g. bread) are baked or toasted.
- **Cellulose** is found in nearly all foods of plant origin. It cannot be digested but can be used as insoluble fibre (dietary fibre).
- **Pectin** is found in most ripe fruits and certain vegetables. It is also extracted and has many commercial uses, mainly as a thickening agent.
- **Glycogen** is formed after digestion and acts as a reserve for a prompt energy requirement. It is converted into glucose when energy is needed.

An **oligosaccharide** is a subset of polysaccharides, containing a small number (typically three to ten) of sugar units, **maltodextrin** for instance. They are used largely as bulking and thickening agents and are present in many sports drinks and (so-called) meal replacement products owing to their low sweetness and high-energy density relative to sucrose. In reality, most foods contain a mixture of both simple and complex carbohydrates.

2.3 Daily carbohydrate intake

A high carbohydrate diet will give a significant increase in performance, so ensuring that pre-exercise glycogen stores are high is essential. It can improve endurance, delay exhaustion, and help you to exercise longer and harder.

- carbohydrate stores - as muscle and liver glycogen - are limited

A popular method for calculating carbohydrate requirements is based on an individual's body mass and his training volume *(see Figure 2.1 below)*. For example, consider a male athlete of 70kg who trains at a medium intensity for an average of 10 hours a week. His carbohydrate needs are thus 6-7g per kg of body mass, so 6 × 70 = 420 and 7 × 70 = 490; hence a daily requirement of about 420-490g of carbohydrates.

Many nutritional sources recommend a daily carbohydrate intake in terms of a percentage of your total daily energy intake, perhaps about 60-70 per cent. However, this can be misleading in terms of optimum nutrition as many athletes have very high energy requirements. If the same person from the previous example needed to consume 4000 calories a day, then 60-70 per cent would mean 640-747g of carbohydrates; way more than is required to maintain muscle glycogen stores. Conversely, those with very low daily energy requirements might not intake enough carbohydrates based on a percentage guide.

Fig 2.1 Daily carbohydrate requirements based on BM and activity

Activity Level	CHO g/kg of BM
Little or no exercise	2 - 3
Light (3-5 hours/week)	3 - 5
Moderate intensity (2-3 hours/day, 5-6 days/week)	5 - 8
High volume/intensity (3-6 hours/day, 5-6 days/week)	8 - 10
Carbohydrate loading for endurance and ultra-endurance events	10 - 12

When referring to the table above bear in mind that the figures are a general guide only, the intensity and individual factor cannot be overstated.

2.4 Carbohydrate absorption

As far as sports performance is concerned, it is how fast the carbohydrates are absorbed from the small intestine into the bloodstream that matters. The faster this occurs the faster the carbohydrates can be taken up by the muscle cells. This makes the difference to performance and recovery, but do not be duped by two very common misconceptions:

- Simple carbohydrates do *not* necessarily imply fast absorption.
- Complex carbohydrates do *not* necessarily imply slow absorption.

2.4.1 Glycaemic index (GI)

The glycaemic index is a measure of how fast you can digest food *and* convert it into glucose. The levels are between 0-100+; slow to fast conversions, respectively. All foods are compared to the reference food, which is pure glucose; rated 100. There are many factors that influence the GI level, such as the particle size, and the amount of starch, fat, protein, sugar and soluble fibre.

GI calculation

1. An amount of test-food containing 50g of carbohydrates is consumed.
2. Over the next 120 minutes, a blood sample is taken every 15 minutes and the blood sugar levels measured.
3. This is calculated as a percentage of your blood sugar level response to 50g of pure glucose (reference food).

Example

Assume your test food is a baked potato. Then you need to eat 250g of baked potatoes to get 50g of carbohydrates because an average baked potato has about 20g of carbohydrate per 100g. Your blood sugar response to the test food is compared with your blood sugar response to the reference food, 50g of glucose. This comparison is given as a percentage; in this case it is about 85 per cent, so the GI of baked potato is 85. Therefore, eating a baked potato (on its own) produces a rise in blood sugar, which is 85 per cent as great as eating pure glucose. Most values lie between 20-100, and many nutritionists categorise food as:

- high (GI 70+)
- medium (GI 56-69)
- low (GI ≤ 55)

However, this is very deceptive as the actual portion size needs to be considered. This is where the **glycaemic *load*** comes in.

2.4.2 Glycaemic load (GL)

The GL gives an idea of the impact a specific portion of a specific food will have on our blood glucose levels. The calculation considers the actual amount of carbohydrates in the serving *and* the glycaemic index. So it factors in both the quantity and the quality of the dietary carbohydrates consumed.

GL = (Dietary CHO in grammes per portion × GI) / 100

At present there seems to be little agreement, and comparatively few papers, on the intake of GL for sports performance. However, the following general nutrition guide is often suggested by nutritionists:

- A typical meal should have a GL of around 20-25, or at least under 30.
- A typical snack should be between 10 and 15.
- In total, your daily GL should be about 100; less than 80 is considered low, and more than 120 is considered high.

For individual foods or meals the levels are:

- low GL = 10 or under
- medium GL = 11-19
- high GL = 20 or above

These figures are all very well, but they seem not to consider a person in training, especially a serious athlete. It is likely therefore that the figures need to be higher - perhaps much higher - so make sure that all your energy needs are met, and in time you should be able to devise a personal table of low-to-high GL levels.

Watermelon is often used as an example when comparing the GI level of a particular food to its GL level. Watermelon has a GI of 72, which is considered high, but its GL level is only 7, which is considered very low. The reason is down to the size of a typical serving - say, about a 150g-slice - which has a very small amount of carbohydrate in it. Consequently the GI has a limited use by itself as it only considers the *speed* of glucose conversion; the GI of, say, one bar of chocolate is exactly the same as 100 bars, 1000 bars, 10,000 bars, and so on.

There have been far more papers on the GI and its effects on exercise than for the GL, but even so, the GI is still considered a relatively new idea and the conclusions on GI with respect to exercise performance do not always agree. However, the more recent papers seem to show that moderate-to-high GI intakes before exercise do have a positive effect on performance.

2.4.3 GI and GL meal calculation

Since we normally eat a combination of foods - i.e., a mixture of some or all of carbohydrate, protein and fat - it is more useful to know the estimated GL of a meal, as opposed to just particular foods. However, for the sake of comparison, both the GI and the GL of the same meal is demonstrated in *Figures 2.2* and *2.3*, respectively.

For the GI of a meal, the carbohydrate value of *each* food item is considered (CHO/g column) as a percentage of the total carbohydrate (% of CHO column) amount of the entire meal. Each of these percentages is used against their respective GI levels to find their GI contribution (last column) to the entire meal. The sum of these individual contributions is what gives the meal its GI value as a whole.

Fig 2.2 GI meal example*

Food item	CHO g	% of CHO	GI	GI contribution to meal
30g Special K	25	(25/57)100 = 44	64	44% of 64 = 28
150ml soya milk	6	(6/57)100 = 11	30	11% of 30 = 3
150ml pure orange juice	13	(13/57)100 = 23	46	23% of 46 = 11
1 slice of toast	13	(13/57)100 = 23	70	23% of 70 = 16
Total CHO g	**57**			**Total meal GI = 58**

*All figures have been rounded to the nearest whole number

Now consider the **GL** of the *same* meal.

Fig 2.3 GL meal example

Food	CHO g	GI	GL contribution to meal
30g Special K	25	64	(25 × 64)/100 = 16
150ml soya milk	6	30	(6 × 30)/100 = 2
150ml pure orange juice	13	46	(13 × 46)/100 = 6
1 slice of toast	13	70	(13 × 70)/100 = 9
Total CHO g	**57**		**Total meal GL = 33**

*All figures have been rounded to the nearest whole number

Notice how the GI at 58 is considered medium by GI standards, yet the GL of the same meal at 33 is considered quite high by GL standards.

2.4.4 Glycaemic intake

High glucose levels cause large amounts of insulin to be produced that causes the excess glucose to be forced into the fat cells. So to optimise glycogen storage and minimise fat storage:

1. eat at regular times and do not overeat
2. avoid carbohydrate overloading
3. keep to balanced combinations of carbohydrates, proteins and good fat.

High glycaemic foods can be consumed, but combine them with protein and/or a little good fat; a baked potato (high GL) with tuna (low GL), for instance. These combinations result in steadier insulin levels and less fat storage. **Both protein and fat slows digestion and hence the release of glucose.**

Exercise modifies the Glycaemic response. Tests have found that when **athletes** are fed high GI foods; they produce far less insulin than would be predicted from GI tables. Hence they do not show the same peaks and troughs in insulin as sedentary people do, so:

- **regard GI tables as a rough guide to how it may affect *your* blood sugar**
- **remember to consider the GL as well**

For an excellent source of information on glycaemic indexes and glycaemic loads see the **Useful websites for sports nutrition**, page 326, **University of Sydney GI and GL website and database**

Fibre

Fibre is a type of carbohydrate that cannot be absorbed by the body - it is not a nutrient and contains no calories or vitamins. There are two types: soluble fibre, which is often called roughage, and insoluble fibre, which is often called dietary fibre.

- **Soluble fibre (roughage)** lowers cholesterol levels and slows down the digestion of carbohydrates, resulting in a slower blood glucose rise. Some rich sources are: apples, barley, oats, pears, strawberries, beans, lentils, rye, and most vegetables.

- **Insoluble fibre (dietary fibre)** helps speed the passage of food from the bowel by making stools soft and bulky, thus helping to prevent constipation and other bowel problems. Some rich sources are wholegrain breads, cereals, rice and pasta, fruits, beans and vegetables.

In general, always aim to get most of your carbohydrates from unrefined and unprocessed foods and bear in mind that fibre modifies the glycaemic effect of a meal in a positive way.

- **The Department of Health (DoH) recommends 18-24g of fibre a day.**

2.5 The carbohydrate cycle

The **carbohydrate cycle refers to the entire fuelling process before, during and after exercise**. A low carbohydrate diet means low muscle and liver glycogen stores, and such diets have shown to reduce the ability to sustain exercise at 70-per-cent VO$_2$ max (i.e., high intensity) for longer than 60 minutes. Low carbohydrate diets have also demonstrated an adverse affect during short maximum power output exercises. Low muscle glycogen will mean a reliance on fat and protein for energy, and protein reliance could mean a loss in lean muscle mass.

2.5.1 Before exercise

It is normally best to eat one to four hours before training, but this of course depends on the individual, what has been consumed, the intensity, how much, and many other factors. A general guide is:

- **not too full and not too hungry for best performance**

A large time gap between eating and training, six or seven hours perhaps, may cause hypoglycaemia (low blood glucose). This causes early fatigue and dizziness and consequently increases the risk of injury. The time range of 1-4 hours allows for the carbohydrate intake to contribute to the glycogen stores of the liver and muscles, especially when a low GL has been consumed.

Carbohydrate intake within an hour before training can cause symptoms of hyper-glycaemia, including fatigue and also gastrointestinal problems. Moreover, a recent study of moderate intensity exercise concluded that there was no beneficial difference between a carbohydrate intake an hour before training and 15 minutes before, so a carbohydrate intake (especially a large amount) very close to your training time seems pointless unless deemed absolutely necessary.

Exercising on an empty stomach

In theory this may encourage burning more fat for fuel than usual, since insulin levels are at their lowest and glucagons are at their highest after a long fast, such as first thing in the morning. This increases the amount of fat that leave your fat cells and travel to your muscles where the fat is burned. However, in practice you are likely to fatigue ear-lier and perform less intensely, which ultimately means burning fewer calories and less fat. If performance is your goal, as opposed to fat loss, exercising on an empty stomach will certainly reduce endurance.

As for strength and muscle building, it is vital to have at least a light meal before exer-cise. An empty stomach means muscle glycogen and blood sugar levels are low, which in turn means the muscles will be forced to burn protein for fuel and consequently you may lose muscle mass.

Pre-exercise carbohydrate intake

The amount of carbohydrate intake and the time gap between intake and exercise is very much an individual thing, but it is worth noting that many athletes suffer from hypoglycaemia if the time gap between carbohydrate intake and exercise is too long; more so than if the intake is too little. A general guide is:

- **1-4g of carbohydrates per kg of BM**

However, it is certainly wise to experiment with the lower end of this range, several times, and long before any event. In general, **pre-exercise carbohydrate levels that**

exceed your normal daily requirements are only necessary for endurance events. For short or medium duration events of high intensity, such as sprints and karate competitions, carbohydrates are used at an increased rate, but even so, your daily intake should already be sufficient. For medium-to-high intensity sports lasting 60-90 minutes, the normal glycogen stores of a well-trained athlete should still be adequate. This includes most team games such as football, cycling competitions of 40-50 kilometres and running from about 10km up to a half marathon.

For high endurance events, glycogen stores can reduce to very low levels, that will inevitably affect performance and may even have an adverse affect on your body and future training *(See **2.7** for information on **carbohydrate loading**).*

It stills seems unclear which GL intake level is the most beneficial to performance - low, medium or high. Some studies show that a low GL gives better endurance, yet others show no significant difference between high or low GL meals before exercise. However, since a low GL is shown to be the same or better with regards to endurance, and generally has a better nutritional content, then a low GL is perhaps best. A high GL is more risky to performance, especially if you are sensitive to blood sugar fluctuations and other problems. In any case, despite the conflicting studies, the more recent ones seem to favour a low GL meal prior to exercise.

As for non-endurance events, a low GL is also better in general for the same reasons as above, but a moderate GL might be best if your intake is close to your training time - say, about 45-75 minutes before, or even 30-60 minutes before if you are doing resistance training. Keep in mind that a high GL taken close to training might cause hyperglycaemia or gastrointestinal problems, whereas a low GL may not provide the required glucose on time.

2.5.2 During exercise

Carbohydrate intake during exercise depends primarily on the duration and the intensity. The reason carbohydrates are taken during a session is to provide necessary fuel at a comfortable level that could not be provided before training.

Duration of 0-60 minutes regardless of intensity

Anything other than water is unnecessary. If you feel a need for extra carbohydrates during this time range, then you probably need to review your pre-exercise intake; the amount, type and timing may all need to be reconsidered.

60+ minutes at moderate-high intensity

Carbohydrate intake will certainly delay fatigue and enable a higher intensity performance, and may allow for continued exercise when your muscle glycogen stores are depleted. After about 60 minutes, muscle glycogen stores dwindle quite significantly, so blood sugar (glucose) comes into major play. As you continue to exercise, the muscles will take more and more glucose from the bloodstream. After two to three hours, the muscles will be fuelled entirely by blood glucose (some of which come from the liver) and fat.

When the liver glycogen stores run low, blood glucose levels fall, and consequently your energy levels as well. This is why temporary hypoglycaemia is common after 2-3 hours of exercise without carbohydrate consumption. Hence, depletion of muscle and liver glycogen, together with low blood sugar levels, cause you to reduce exercise intensity or stop completely. Therefore, consumption of additional carbohydrates during exercise would maintain blood sugar levels and allow for longer exercise and a far better performance.

30-60g of carbohydrates per hour is commonly recommended, and this makes sense (at least theoretically), since the maximum amount of carbohydrate that the body can oxidise is believed to be about 1g a minute (i.e., about 60g/hour). Therefore, **over consumption will neither improve your energy output nor reduce fatigue**.

Carbohydrate consumption must take place before fatigue sets in, and since it normally takes at least 30 minutes for carbohydrates just to be absorbed into the bloodstream, they should be consumed early in your session, especially if you know your routine is going to be hard and for a long time. However, research has shown that performance is still improved and fatigue delayed even when carbohydrates are consumed relatively late in the event.

Recommended types of carbohydrates

Carbohydrates consumed during exercise should be easy to digest and absorb; you need it to raise your blood sugar levels and reach your exercising muscles rapidly. Liquid carbohydrates are more convenient, and also contain much-needed fluids. Solid carbohydrates are equally good for performance, but are less convenient, and need to be taken with fluids anyway. Research has shown that protein co-ingested with carbohydrate may have added benefits over carbohydrates alone, especially with regard to muscle protein synthesis. **The recommended ratio of carbohydrates to protein is 4:1.**

Ideas of comestibles during exercise providing 30g carbohydrates:

- 500ml isotonic sports drink (6g/100ml)
- homemade diluted fluids (*see* **Chapter 6**)
- 40g raisins or sultanas
- 1-2 bananas

2.5.3 Post exercise

The length of time that it takes to refuel depends on four main factors:

- how depleted your glycogen stores are after exercise
- the extent of muscle damage
- the amount of carbohydrate you eat and the timing
- your training experience and fitness level

The more depleted your glycogen stores, the longer it will take to refuel, but it also depends on the intensity and duration of your exercise.

Intensity influence

During explosive exercise or high-intensity aerobics, most of your energy will be provided for by your muscle and liver glycogen stores, far more than for low-intensity activities of equal duration. As exercise intensity increases so does the amount of energy contributed by glycogen. The mode of exercise is also a major factor when considering the effects of post-exercise glycogen replenishment. Eccentric exercise, for instance, can take up to four days for glycogen replenishment, significantly longer than for aerobic training. In exercise, the term *eccentric* refers to the lowering phase of a movement, such as lowering a dumbbell during a curl. There are three phase of muscle/tendon movement, the other two are isometric (no movement) and concentric (muscle contraction). The term *eccentric training* (or exercise) is based on slowing down the eccentric movement of an exercise.

In general, at least 20 hours are required to replenish muscle glycogen stores, even with a carefully selected diet, so athletes who train two or more times a day need to give their glycogen replenishment special attention.

Duration influence

The duration of your exercise also has a bearing on the amount of glycogen you use. For instance, if you run for one hour, you will use up more glycogen than if you ran for half an hour at the same speed. If you complete 10 sets of shoulder presses, you will use more glycogen from your shoulder muscles than if you had completed only five sets at the same mass. This might appear glaringly obvious, but many athletes do not adjust their refuelling intake accordingly.

- **You must allow more time to refuel after high-intensity or long workouts.**

Post-exercise carbohydrate intake

Replace your glycogen stores as soon as it is comfortably possible post-exercise. Replenishment is fastest within the first two hours, but the sooner the better. Between two and four hours after training, the replenishment will still be faster than normal, but half as quick as within the immediate two hours post-training:

- **Take 50-75g of carbohydrates as soon as possible after training, certainly within the 45 minutes immediately after training.**
- **Continue at a rate of 1-1.5g per kg BM for the next few hours or until your next meal.**

For example, a 70kg person would need to ingest 70-135g of carbohydrates for the next few hours after training, in addition to the initial 50-75g. Even if you finish your training late in the evening, you still need to start the refuelling process; do not go to bed on an empty stomach after training, as it will delay replenishment, and may cause muscle damage.

A number of papers have shown that carbohydrates ingested with protein and a little fat hastens the rate of glycogen synthesis when compared to carbohydrate intake alone. Moreover, after resistance training such co-ingestion has not only shown a faster glycogen synthesis but also a more efficient muscle growth.

- **CHO to protein at a ratio of 4:1**

A moderate-to-high GL is best, since it is necessary to get glucose into the bloodstream as quickly as possible.

Post-exercise snack ideas

The list below suggests some ideas for post exercise snacks, but you will need to check the levels of carbohydrate, protein and fat to ensure that you are getting the right amounts, especially for carbohydrates. Some items below suggest a milk alternative; these include soya milk, oat milk and rice milk. If a lack of appetite or gastric discomfort occurs soon after exercise be sure to avoid high fibre foods and review your pre-exercise and during-exercise carbohydrate intakes:

- 1-2 portions of fresh fruit with a glass of milk or milk alternative
- 1-2 cartons of yoghurt
- homemade fresh-fruit shake made with milk or milk alternative
- wholemeal sandwich with protein filling
- a handful of nuts and dried fruit
- a bowl of porridge made with a milk or milk alternative

Efficiency in refuelling improves with training experience and fitness levels. It takes a beginner longer to replace glycogen stores than an experienced athlete eating the same amount of carbohydrates; this is part of the reason that experienced athletes are able to train almost every day, whilst beginners cannot, or at least, should not. Another advantage that the experienced athlete has is the ability to store a higher amount of glycogen, perhaps by as much as 20 per cent more.

2.6 Training and immunity

More and more research suggests that consistent moderate exercise boosts your immune system; partly by a temporary boost in the production of macrophages, the cells that attack bacteria. Furthermore, during moderate exercise, immune cells circulate through the body more quickly and are thus able to kill bacteria and viruses more easily. Although the immune system tends to return to normal within a few hours post exercise, regular moderate exercise seems to makes these immune-boosting changes last a little longer.

Conversely, too much high-intensity exercise can temporarily reduce the production of immune cells, thus making the athlete more susceptible to colds and infections. In particular, research has shown this to be the case for the first 72 hours after more than 90 minutes of high-intensity exercise, so high-endurance and high-intensity athletes are particularly at risk.

During such exercise the body produces stress hormones, such as cortisol and adrenaline, which raise blood pressure and cholesterol levels. The following advice may help prevent or lessen the affects of exercise-related immunity suppression:

- Ensure you include adequate recovery time, especially after ultra-endurance events, to allow your immunity to recuperate.
- If you feel run down or have any symptoms of over-training, such as a raised heart rate, irritability or fatigue, you need to slow down or stop your training temporarily.
- If you are already ill you may need to recover before you resume training. If you have a mild cold but no fever, moderate exercise might help, but anything more than this might make you worse.
- Ensure your energy intake is sufficient; under-eating will increase cortisol levels.
- Consume plenty of wholesome foods (*see 7.2, page 163*).
- Avoid low-carbohydrate diets, because this leads to low glycogen stores, which in turn increases cortisol levels and consequently suppresses the immune cells.

- Make sure you consume the 30-60g carbohydrates an hour during intense exercise if required. This can reduce stress hormone levels.
- Drink adequate fluids *(see **Chapter 6, Fluid Essentials**).*
- A vitamin/mineral supplement may be useful *(see 7.6).*

2.7 Carbohydrate loading

The idea of carbohydrate loading is to increase muscle glycogen stores to above normal levels. With more glycogen available you ought to be able to exercise for longer before fatigue sets in. This is potentially advantageous in endurance events lasting longer than 90 minutes continuously, but unlikely to benefit you if your event is less than 90 minutes, since muscle glycogen depletion will not normally hinder your performance within this time period.

Events that last less than 90 minutes should normally be suitably fuelled by your general daily carbohydrate intake. However, if you feel that this is not the case, then aim to intake 5-10g of carbohydrates per kg of body mass 24-36 hours prior to the event. You should also decrease or even stop training during this 24-36-hour pre-event period in order to save your glycogen.

For endurance events of more than 90 minutes, the loading period should begin 36-72 hours before the event, with carbohydrate levels at 7-12g per kg of body mass. Training during, the loading period should gradually decrease and perhaps cease altogether on the penultimate day, whilst the carbohydrate intake should gradually increase during this period. The level to which the training decreases is difficult to state exactly, but many feel that the intensity and time allowed for training should lower significantly. Many carbohydrate loading regimens offer explicit advice by detailing each day's recommendations for the entire loading phase. This is very convenient but has the fundamental drawback of not considering the athlete as an individual.

It is worth remembering that each gramme of glycogen is stored with about 3-4g of water, and consequently carbohydrate loading can increase your BM by about 1-2kg. This is well worth bearing in mind, since a BM increase may affect your performance, and in some sports may also mean that you have exceeded a given weight limit. The best advice is trial and error, but never try anything new just before an important event. Always allow plenty of time to establish what works best for you as far in advance as possible. It is best to try several individual carbohydrate loading programmes long before any major event.

3 PROTEINS

Protein is a large complex molecule made up of one or more chains of amino acids. Protein makes up part of the structure of every cell and tissue in the body, including muscle tissue, internal organs, tendons, skin, hair, and nails; on average it comprises about 20 per cent of your body mass. Protein is required for the growth and formation of new tissue, tissue repair, and can be used as fuel for energy production. It is also needed to make almost all of the body's enzymes and has numerous other important roles, way beyond the scope of this book. This chapter discusses the fundamentals of amino acids (the building blocks of protein), the main protein types and the absorbability of protein in general. The distinct intakes of protein depending on the individuals' activity and body mass are also addressed, as well as the much-debated role of protein in muscle-building and weight control.

3.1 Protein storage

Protein is not stored in the same way as carbohydrates and fats, it is mainly used as building material for muscle and organ tissue. ATP production during most forms of exercise comes mainly from broken-down carbohydrates and fats. **Protein is broken down for energy when glycogen stores have become depleted**, and thus plays an important role during the later stages of very intense or very long exercise.

3.2 Amino acids

Amino acids are organic molecules that form **the building blocks of protein**. Most organisms construct protein from a particular set of 20 amino acids, hence why most sources refer to the 20 amino acids, although several dozen other amino acids are found in nature. They can be combined in various ways to form hundreds of different proteins in the body. When you eat protein it is broken down in the digestive tract into smaller molecular units - single amino acids and dipeptides (two amino acids linked together).

Twelve amino acids can be made in the body via other amino acids, carbohydrates and nitrogen. These are called Dispensable Amino Acids (**DAA**), i.e. non-essential amino acids. The other eight are called Indispensable Amino Acids (**IAA**), i.e. they must be provided via the diet. To be precise, some of the so-called DAA, such as histidine and cysteine, are sometimes called semi-essential amino acids because the ability of children to synthesize them is not fully developed.

DAA	IAA
Alanine	Isoleucine (BCAA)
Arginine	Leucine (BCAA)
Asparagine	Lysine
Aspartic acid	Methionine
Cysteine	Phenylalanine
Glutamic acid	Threonine
Glutamine	Tryptophan
Glycine	Valine (BCAA)
Histidine	
Proline	
Serine	
Tyrosine	

Branched-chain amino acids

Branched-chain amino acids (**BCAA**) include the three IAA which have a branched molecular shape: valine, leucine and isoleucine. These make up one-third of the protein in muscle tissue, and are a vital **substrate** (in this case: a molecule on which an enzyme acts) for glutamine and alanine which are released in large quantities during increased aerobic exercise. Unlike other amino acids, they are metabolised in the muscle, as opposed to the liver. They can also be used as a fuel by the muscles, especially when muscle glycogen is depleted. In fact, the body's requirement is for amino acids rather than protein.

Protein metabolism

DAA and IAA accumulate in the liver and blood, the so-called *amino acid pool*. From here the amino acids have one of four fates; they can be:

- used to build new protein
- oxidised to produce energy
- converted into fatty acid or glucose
- excreted, in part, in urine or perhaps sweat

3.2.1 Protein types

There are four main types of protein commonly used as food supplements:

- **Whey protein**: from curdled milk, the whey is separated from the curd. This is good post exercise because it digests quickly (about 30 minutes).
- **Casein**: the curd, when milk is separated into curds and whey. This is digested very slowly (2-7 hours). Muscle builders often take this before bedtime since this is normally the longest period that the body is not supplied with any protein.
- **Soy protein**: from soya beans. This is not absorbed as efficiently as whey or egg protein, but it is believed by many nutritionists to have numerous health benefits in general.
- **Egg protein (albumen)**: from whole eggs. This is digested at a relatively medium pace (1.5-3 hours) and is therefore used at any time for a sustained release of amino acids in the body.

Blended proteins, a combination of any or all of the above, are also popular, especially among muscle builders. The idea is that you get all the desired digestion rates; hence, you can take the protein at any time and still get fast, medium, and slow absorptions.

3.3 Protein and exercise

Numerous studies (for both endurance and strength exercise) have shown that the recommended protein of **0.8g/kg of body mass** is inadequate for those involved in regular training. Additional protein is needed to compensate for the increased breakdown of protein during and after exercise. The greater the intensity and the longer the duration of exercise, the more protein is broken down for fuel. So the requirement depends on many factors, including type, intensity, and duration of exercise (*see the table below for intake suggestions*).

Fig 3.1.Protein requirement against exercise type

Exercise type and intensity	Daily protein intake per kg of BM
Sedentary	0.8g
General training	1.0g
Endurance - heavy training	1.2-1.6g
Endurance - extreme training	2.0g
Strength and power - heavy training	1.2-1.7g
Fat-loss programme	1.6g
Weight-gain programme*	1.8-2.0g

*(see *also* **8.1, Protein** *and* **9.4, Weight-gain supplements**)

According to research, a **protein intake above your optimal requirements will not result in further muscle mass and strength**.

3.3.1 Endurance

Prolonged and intense endurance training increases the protein requirement for two main reasons:

1. More protein is required to compensate for the increased breakdown of protein during exercise. When muscle glycogen stores are low (typically after 60-90 minutes of endurance exercise), certain amino acids can be used for energy. Protein may contribute up to 15 per cent of your energy when glycogen stores are low. When muscle glycogen stores are high, protein contributes less than 5 per cent of energy needs.
2. Additional protein is needed for the repair and recovery of muscle tissue after intense endurance needs.

3.3.2 Strength and power

Strength and power athletes require additional protein since it helps stimulate muscle growth. To build muscle, you must be in **positive nitrogen balance**, in other words, the body must retain more dietary protein than it excretes or uses as fuel. Otherwise, the result could be slower gains in muscle mass and in strength, or even muscle loss, irrespective of how hard you train. However, the body does adapt to varying amounts of protein intake. For low amounts it adapts by becoming more efficient with what is supplied. For high amounts it will oxidise the surplus amino acids for energy. Nonetheless, these are not good reasons to under- or over-supply your protein intake.

3.3.4 Novice athletes and protein

Contrary to popular belief, studies have shown that **beginners have a slightly higher protein requirement**. When you begin a training programme, your protein needs are higher because of an increase in protein turnover. However, as mentioned above, the body adapts, and after about three weeks of the new training regime it becomes more efficient at using protein.

3.4 Protein and consumption

Protein comes mainly from meat and fish, dairy products and eggs, nuts and seeds, pulses, soya products, and grains and cereals.

3.4.1 Protein bioavailability

This is a term used by several branches of scientific study - originally from pharmacology - to refer to the way chemicals are absorbed by humans and other animals. In terms of sports nutrition, it refers to the *usefulness* of the protein food or supplement. Foods that contain all eight IAA are sometimes called **complete proteins** (or whole proteins). In fact, most foods that contain protein include all 20 amino acids, but there are still many that are lacking in one or more of the IAAs.

Protein digestibility correct amino acid (PDCAA) score

This refers to a method for evaluating the protein quality of a food with respect to amino acids required by humans. Each food has a rating, one being the highest and zero the lowest:

- whey (1.0)
- egg white (1.0)
- casein (1.0)
- milk (1.0)
- soy protein isolates (1.0)
- beef (0.92)
- soya beans (0.91)
- vegetables (0.74)
- legumes in general (0.69)
- kidney beans (0.68)
- rye (0.68)
- cereals (0.58)
- whole wheat (0.54)
- lentils (0.52)
- peanuts (0.52)

Unfortunately there are several methods for measuring how readily used a protein is, such as the Biological Value (BV), Net Protein Utilisation (NPU) and the Protein Efficiency Ratio (PER). However, it seems that of these the Biological Value is currently most popular, especially amongst strength athletes.

Biological Value

The bioavailability of a protein is often measured by its Biological Value (BV), the proportion of absorbed protein. The BV indicates how readily a broken down protein can be used in protein synthesis. There are two ways to measure a food's BV, percentage utilisation and relative utilisation. By convention, the percentage utilisation uses the per cent (%) suffix, and the relative utilisation uses no unit.

Percentage utilisation is a simple ratio of N_r, the nitrogen incorporated into the body on the test diet, and N_a, the nitrogen absorbed in proteins on the test diet. The value can be 100 per cent or less, including negative values, which are possible if the nitrogen excreted is greater than the protein intake. A BV of 100 per cent means a complete utilisation of dietary protein. The formula is given by:

$$BV = (N_r/N_a)100$$

Relative protein is a measure against an easily utilised protein, normally egg protein, as this is considered the easiest protein to utilise. Egg protein is effectively the gold standard and is given a relative BV of 100, the highest value of all foods, and hence a high proportion of egg protein is used for making new bodily proteins. Two tests are carried out on the same individual, one with the test protein and one with the reference protein, egg protein. The formula is given by:

$$\text{Relative BV} = (BV_{test}/BV_{egg})100$$

Unlike the percentage utilisation, the relative utilisation can be above 100; for example, whey protein has a relative BV of 104. Egg protein, incidentally, has a percentage utilisation BV of 93.7 per cent. In any case, such comparisons should be treated in context as the test methods are quite different, so converting between the two should only be taken as a rough guide.

The main advantage of using the relative BV measure, as opposed to the percentage utilisation, is that it takes into account an individual's metabolism, and is therefore more accurate.

Dairy products, meat, fish, poultry, quorn and soya have a relatively **high BV**, 70-100, whereas, nuts, seeds, pulses and grains have a relatively **low BV**, less than 70. Some of the higher valued food items are listed below.

Food item	Relative BV
Whey protein	104
Egg protein	100
Cow's milk	91
Beef	80
Casein	77
Soy	74

Despite the popularity of the BV measure, it is the PDCAA that is universally recognised by many professional bodies, such as the World Health Organisation (WHO), the Food and Drug Administration (FDA), the United Nations University, and the National Academy of Sciences. Furthermore, the BV has more than its fair share of criticism. For instance, the BV of whey protein may be completely misleading because most of it may in fact be used for energy production rather than protein synthesis. The use of rats to determine protein quality and the fact that the BV is relative to the amount of protein given, are among several other issues that have brought disapproval.

3.4.2 Over-consumption of protein

Consuming more than you need has no advantage in terms of health or physical performance. Some protein is converted into glucose for immediate use or is normally stored as glycogen. However, if you are already supplying yourself with enough good-quality carbohydrates (as you should be) to refill your glycogen stores, then in theory, excess glucose may be converted into fat. However, eating protein seems to increase the metabolic rate, so a slight excess of your individual protein needs is unlikely to be converted into a significant amount of fat, if any.

Too much protein may cause undue stress on the liver and kidneys, so those with renal or liver problems are generally advised to consume a low-protein diet. Research has shown that extra water is drawn from the body's fluids to dilate and excrete the increased quantities of urea (the nitrogen-containing amino acid group). Other research counters this by showing that a simple increase in fluid intake will offset this potential problem.

3.4.3 Protein and weight loss
A higher protein intake can offset some of the muscle-wasting effects associated with weight-loss programmes. Researchers recommend a further increase of about 0.2g/kg of body mass. So an endurance (heavy-training) athlete would need 1.4-1.8g/kg and a strength (power) athlete would need as much as 1.4-1.9g/kg. Whichever you choose, keep in mind the potential drawbacks of too much or too little protein.

3.4.5 Vegetarian athletes
We make the assumption that a *vegetarian* does not eat meat, poultry or fish. This being the case, then attaining the daily amounts of protein required for muscle growth and strength, 1.4-1.8g/kg body mass, could be a little difficult. The key is to obtain the correct combinations of such foods, since plant sources generally contain lower amounts of IAA than meat. A mixture of dairy products, pulses, grains, nuts and seeds, quorn and soya products should make it simple enough to get all the required amino acids. Some good combinations are: whole-wheat pasta with chickpeas, beans on wholemeal toast, and lentil soup with a wholemeal roll.

4 Fats

Fats consist of a large group of compounds and can be either solid or liquid at normal room temperature; lipids refer to both liquid and solid fats. There are many different types of fats, but each is a variation of the same chemical structure that normally comprises chains of carbon, hydrogen and oxygen atoms.

This chapter discusses fat storage and the desirable and undesirable fat percentages of people according to age and gender, and also includes the much neglected issues of too little fat and body composition; particular fat percentages according to the sport are also discussed. Cholesterol is briefly covered, as well as the much talked-about body mass index (BMI) and its distinct limitations. The various means and devices of measuring fat percentage are discussed in detail, and the chapter closes with a look at the different types of fat found in food.

4.1 Fat storage

Fat is stored in almost every region of the body, but mainly around the organs and under the skin. Some sources say that about 300-400g of fat is stored in muscles, but these figures are vague, as we shall see.

Essential fat

Essential fat is required for normal physiological functioning, and is found in brain tissue, bone marrow, and in the liver, spleen, heart and several other places.

- In healthy average men, essential fat accounts for about 3-5 per cent of total body mass.
- In healthy average women, essential fat accounts for about 8-12 per cent of total body mass

The extra essential fat for women is necessary for childbearing and other hormonal functions.

Storage fat

Storage fat is spread throughout the body as **subcutaneous fat**, under the skin, and as **visceral fat** (also called intra-abdominal fat), which is fat around the internal organs. Incidentally, storage fat in the abdominal area that is under the skin but not behind the abdominal wall is also subcutaneous fat. The main purpose of storage fat is to protect the organs, provide heat, and act as an energy reserve, and it is storage fat that over-weight people usually need to reduce. The storage continues whether we need it or not, and if it is not burned off it stays there and will continue to accumulate.

- In healthy average men, storage fat accounts for about 12 per cent of total body mass.
- In healthy average women, storage fat accounts for about 15 per cent of total body mass.

The above standard figures suggest that total fat, essential plus storage fat, accounts for 15-17 per cent of total body mass in average healthy men, and 22-27 per cent in average healthy women. As usual, such standard figures can be very misleading. For instance, a 19-year-old woman might think her 26 per cent fat percentage is under average, but in fact it is over average for someone of her age group, and of course these figures do not necessarily account for sports people. The tables below (Fig 4.1 and 4.2) is just one example that you might find on the Internet; it gives a far better idea on fat percentage and its meaning, including the frequently neglected information on too little fat, but is typically unverifiable. Such examples are many, and even though the source cannot be verified (or is at least elusive), the advice may still be good. Unfortunately, such tables are not consistent, some may refer to a particular fat percentage as within a healthy range, where others might classify the same percentage as in an overweight range. Not only this, but they do not cater for athletes or even for those from different parts of the world; the classifications of fat percentages are not the same for all peoples.

Fig 4.1 Male fat percentage ratings

Males	Fat percentage and their rating					
Age range	Too low	Obese	Overweight (excess fat)	Average - healthy	Good	Excellent
20 - 29	< 8	> 26	21 - 26	16 - 20	12 - 15	8 - 11
30 - 39	< 8	> 28	23 - 28	18 - 22	14 - 17	8 - 13
40 - 49	< 11	> 29	24 - 29	19 - 23	15 - 18	11 - 14
50 - 59	< 11	> 30	25 - 30	20 - 24	16 - 19	11 - 15
60 - 69	< 13	> 30	26 - 30	21 - 25	18 - 20	13 - 17
70 - 79	< 15	> 30	27 - 30	22 - 26	20 - 22	15 - 19
80+	< 17	> 30	28 - 30	24 - 27	22 - 24	17 - 21

Fig 4.2 Female fat percentage ratings

Females	Fat percentage and their rating					
Age range	Too low	Obese	Overweight	Average	Good	Excellent
20 - 29	< 18	> 32	25 - 32	23 - 24	20 - 22	18 - 19
30 - 39	< 19	> 33	28 - 33	26 - 27	23 - 25	19 - 22
40 - 49	< 21	> 34	29 - 34	27 - 28	24 - 26	21 - 23
50 - 59	< 23	> 36	31 - 36	29 - 30	26 - 28	23 - 25
60 - 69	< 24	>38	33 - 38	31 - 32	27 - 30	24 - 26
70 - 79	< 24	>38	34 - 38	32 - 33	28 - 31	24 - 27
80+	< 25	>38	35 - 38	33 - 34	29 - 32	25 - 28

A common guide for fat percentages is that suggested by the World Health Organization (WHO) and the National Institutes of Health (NIH), which is based on a paper that was published in 2000. At the time there were no papers that offered suggested fat percentage ranges, despite international interest in the subject. However, this paper was based on finding a link between the BMI *(see section 4.2)* and predicted percentage body fat, so it is a little surprising that since then not much work in this area seems to have been carried out. The accuracy and reliability of the BMI has been called into question for many years, and several large studies over recent years have exposed its limitations and shortcomings, so it would seem natural to 'untie' the link between the BMI and fat percentage and seek an alternative. As it is then, such tables should be accepted as nothing more than a rough guide; the WHO/NIH tables are given below.

Fig 4.3 WHO/NIH - male fat percentage ratings

Age (years)	Too little	Healthy range	Overweight	Obese
20 - 40	< 8	8 - 19	19 - 25	> 25
41 - 60	< 11	11 - 22	22 - 27	> 27
61 - 79	< 13	13 - 25	25 - 30	> 30

Fig 4.4 WHO/NIH - female fat percentage ratings

Age (years)	Too little	Healthy range	Overweight	Obese
20 - 40	< 21	21 - 33	33 - 39	> 39
41 - 60	< 23	23 - 35	35 - 40	> 40
61 - 79	<24	24 - 36	36 - 42	> 42

As for children and teenagers, fat percentage is perhaps only of great concern if it is very high or very low. The following is just a guide for those between the ages of 12 and 19; as for younger children it is best to consult a professional if you have any concerns.

Fig 4.5 Youth fat percentage ratings

Boys' fat percentage	Rating	Girls' fat percentage
25+	Obese	32+
21 - 24	Overweight	22 - 31
16 - 21	Average	14 - 21
9 - 15	Healthy	
< 9	Too low (underweight)	< 14

4.1.1 Sport specific

Some suggest that male athletes should, in general, aim for 6-15 per cent total body fat for peak performance, and female athletes 12-18 per cent total body fat. However, this is for peak performance and therefore may not always be good for health. Physiologists tell us that the minimum fat percentage to keep good health is 5 per cent total body fat for men and 12 per cent total body fat for women. Yet these figures are merely the upper figures of the suggested requirements of essential body fat, thus leaving no room for storage fat, and consequently no energy reserve. Even if your best performance relies on such low body fat percentages, it is inadvisable. Maintaining such low fat levels may, in the end, have a reverse affect on your performance and can lead to an obsession, which in turn often lead to some type of eating disorder. See chapter 10 for more details on eating disorders.

There are even suggestions for desired fat percentages according to particular sports, and many are within, or cross into, a relatively safe range:

- men: tennis (12-16 %), football (8-18%), basketball (7-12 %)
- women: tennis (22-26%), weightlifting (17-20 %), basketball (18-27%)

However, many sports also desire unhealthy, or border on unhealthy, fat levels; these are often the aesthetic sports or those that include weight categories:

- men: bodybuilding (6-7%), gymnastics (3-6%), certain swimming activities (4-10%)
- women: bodybuilding (8-10%), gymnastics (8-18%), certain swimming activities (12-15%)
- recommended body fat levels are 13-18% for men
- recommended body fat levels are 18-25% for women

In any case, fat percentage suggestions for particular sports are far from established, and it seems that the suggestions are little more than educated guesses. Despite the easily-obtainable fat percentage guides for specific sports, available on the Internet and in many magazines and books, none seems to come with references to reliable sources of information. However, this should be no surprise, deciding on which is the best fat percentage for just one sport would be incredibly difficult to do fairly, as well as time-consuming and costly; so educated guesses and trial-and-error are perhaps forgivable in most cases.

Certainly athletes tend to border on the lower end of the 'safe' range of body fat percentages without detriment to their health, but it seems that there is no benefit for male athletes to drop below 8 per cent body fat, and female athletes to drop below 14 per cent. Nonetheless, these figures are still quite low, so if you are close to these it is strongly advisable to at least have a consultation with a sport physician.

Dangers of very low body fat

Many studies have shown that if a man's total body fat falls below five per cent, testosterone levels will fall, affecting libido and causing a sharp fall in sperm count. The problem though, is quickly and easily rectified once body fat increases again.

Very low fat levels have a far greater effect on women, especially if overtraining as well; one of the main problems being hormone imbalance and amenorrhoea - a complete cessation of periods. The levels vary from one woman to another, but these adverse effects tend to happen once the fat levels fall below, or sometimes within, the 15-20 per cent range for women 20 years old and above.

Another major concern of amenorrhoea is that it can lead to bone loss. This is because oestrogen loss leads to mineral loss in the bones, and this means a loss in bone density. The bones become lighter, thinner and thus far more fragile, making them more susceptible to stress fractures and other problems. The good news is that all quickly returns to normal soon after fat levels increase and the training overload is decreased (*see also* **Chapter 10, Women in Training**).

4.1.2 Cholesterol

Cholesterol is a particular type of fat that is an essential part of our body; it is found in cell membranes and several hormones. Some of it comes from our diet, but most is made in the liver from saturated fats. If we eat more, the liver produces less to compensate, but if we eat less, the liver makes more to compensate - this way a steady stream of cholesterol is kept in the bloodstream. However, when people become obese, do little or no exercise, and eat so much saturated fat that an imbalance occurs and health suffers, it is this *imbalance* that is the problem rather than cholesterol itself.

There are harmful and protective lipoproteins, commonly called 'bad' and 'good' cholesterol, these are: low-density lipoprotein (LDL) and high-density lipoprotein (HDL), respectively. LDL carries cholesterol from your liver to the cells in the body that need it, but if there is too much, it may harden the archery walls, which may lead to heart disease. HDL, on the other hand, carries cholesterol away from the cells back to the liver, which is then broken down and excreted as waste. A simple blood test, called a **lipoprotein profile**, is used to measure cholesterol levels; you will need to fast for about 12 hours before. This test gives information on your:

- total cholesterol
- LDL
- HDL
- triglycerides (another form of fat in your blood)

The cholesterol levels and their categories with respect to health are tabulated below.

Fig 4.6 Cholesterol levels

Total cholesterol level	Category
Less than 200mg/dL	Desirable
200 - 239mg/dL	Borderline high
240mg/dL or greater	Too high
LDL cholesterol level - often called bad cholesterol	
Less than 100mg/dL	Optimal
100 - 129mg/dL	Near optimal - above optimal
HDL cholesterol level - often called good cholesterol	
Less than 40mg/dL	Too low
40 - 59mg/dL	Okay, but higher is better
60 + mg/dL	Considered protective against heart disease
Triglyceride level	
Less than 150mg/dL	Normal

If you prefer, you can have just your **total cholesterol and HDL levels** measured - which does not require any fasting - and it is a ratio of these two figures that is commonly quoted as one's cholesterol level. Nevertheless, if your total cholesterol level is more than 200mg/dL (milligrammes per decilitre), or if your HDL is less than 40mg/dL, you will need a lipoprotein profile done.

The amount of **cholesterol present in the blood can range from 3.6 to 7.8mmol/Litre**, where greater than 6 mmol/L is considered as too high and is a risk factor for arterial disease. The UK government recommends a target of less than 5mmol/L, but at present the average man in the UK has a cholesterol level of 5.5 mmol/L and the average woman has an average level of 5.6 mmol/L. The ratio used is:

- **total cholesterol/HDL**

For example, using a borderline-high total cholesterol level of 230 and a low HDL level of 38, the cholesterol level would be:

total cholesterol/HDL = 230/38 = 6.1 (too high)

4.2 Body Mass Index (BMI)

This is a clinical measure often used to estimate weight classification with regards to health risks; it is sometimes known as the Quetelet Index, after its inventor Adolphe Quetelet. The calculation is as follows:

- Your mass in kg /your height (in metres) squared

For example, the BMI of a person weighing 70kg who is 1.7m tall is calculated as follows:

70 / (1.7 × 1.7) = 24 (2 s.f.)

According to the BMI table below (***Fig. 4.7***) this puts this person just inside the normal weight category.

Some books also give reference to a BMI grade zero, but this is omitted here as the grades only really relate to *levels of obesity*. Most sources do not include the extra *waist size* information, but it is very important since this gives a clearer picture of risk classification.

Figure 4.7 BMI classification

BMI number, x	Classification	Grade	Health risks according to waist (W) size, for males (m) and females (f)	
			W ≤ 40 ins (m), W ≤ 35 ins (f)	W 40 ins (m) W 35 ins (f)
$x < 16.5$	Severely underweight	n/a	n/a	n/a
$16.5 \le x < 18.5$	Underweight	n/a	n/a	n/a
$18.5 \le x < 25$	Normal, healthy	n/a	n/a	n/a
$25 \le x < 30$	Overweight	n/a	Increased	High
$30 \le x < 35$	Obese (moderately)	I	High	Very high
$35 \le x < 40$	Obese (mod-high)	II	Very high	Very high
$x \ge 40$	Morbidly obese	III	Extremely high	Extremely high

Though the BMI is widely used by health and sport professionals, it has been heavily criticised, especially since it does not take into consideration a person's fat-to-muscle ratio - of particular interest to sports people - or frame size, water weight, varying degrees of bone density and so on. Even so, the BMI is still be a reasonable measure for classifying individuals as underweight, normal/healthy, overweight or obese, but is not a useful tool for athletes, children, the elderly or infirm.

Moreover, BMI classifications are not the same in all countries or among peoples; Asians, Caucasians, Africans and so on, all have distinct body types and distinct distributions and amounts of body fat. For example, the table below (*Fig 4.8*) is based on a Japanese study in 2007. You will notice that a BMI of 23 would be classified as overweight for a Japanese person, yet figure 4.7 would classify this as normal/healthy.

Fig 4.8 A Japanese BMI classification

BMI	Classification
18.5 - 22.9	Normal
23 - 24.9	Overweight
25+	Obese

For a BMI specific to your age, gender, mass, height and ethnicity, see the **BMI** link on page 327.

Differing BMI tables

Some BMI tables will seemingly differ only slightly from figure 4.7 above, but these slight differences can make for significantly different results. In some tables the underweight BMI starts at below 20, not below 18.5, as in our table. Yet this is quite a difference because a person who is 1.7 m tall would need to weigh just below 53.5kg to be classed as underweight according to our table, whereas they would need to weigh just under 57.8kg to be classed as underweight if *underweight* was set at a BMI of less than 20 - a difference of over 4kg. This difference is not small, so care should be taken when referring to BMI levels. Some tables are also divided into fewer categories; this often means a single range from 30 to 40, i.e. no distinction between Grades I and II of obesity.

Deceptive BMI ranges

Do not be deceived by the seemingly small ranges involved in BMI calculations, as these small ranges allow for a large range in mass. The table below demonstrates this by showing the potential BMI of a person who is 1.78 m tall.

Figure 4.9 BMI ranges for a person who is 1.78m tall

Classification	Mass range
Underweight	Below 58.6kg
Normal	58.6 - 79.2kg
Overweight	79.2 - 95kg
Obese grade I	95 - 111kg
Obese grade II	111 - 127kg
Obese grade III	Above 127kg

To bring home the point, consider a man who is 1.75 metres tall with a BMI of 27, just two above normal. This means that this particular person has a mass of 82.7kg. Since he needs to be just below a BMI of 25 to be just inside the normal/healthy range, he would need to reduce his mass to just less than 75.6kg. Hence, in his case, a BMI of just two above normal implies that he is at least 7kg overweight.

As discussed earlier in this chapter, fat percentages are far from perfect, just refer to any of figures 4.1 to 4.5 and you will notice that a *healthy* or an *excellent* fat percentage is knocking on the door of *too low*. Nonetheless, with further research the figures will become more agreeable and the methods of measuring them more accurate. As for the BMI, it seems clear that after some 160 years, it is perhaps approaching the end of its use.

Desired BMIs

Some people may want to know what body mass they need to have for a particular BMI. For instance, an athlete who is 1.74m tall and who has a BM of 78kg has a BMI of 25.8 (overweight), might wish to know what his BM needs to be for him to have a BMI of 23 (normal/healthy). The equation is omitted here, but such questions can be answered by using the corresponding Excel program.

4.3 Body composition

It is important to understand the term *body composition*, since this will explain the difference between having excessive fat and being (so-called) overweight; they are not necessarily the same thing. The body, loosely speaking, can be divided into two parts:

- bone and lean tissue
- body fat (adipose tissue)

The term body composition refers to your proportion of these two elements, where lean body tissue includes the muscles, body organs, blood and so on. For good health we should aim to gain an improved balance between these two parts, our body composition. This means that it is not our mass that accurately informs us if we are in good condition, but rather our lean muscle-to-fat ratio. Two people - same gender, age, height, etc. - could weigh the same yet have completely contrasting body compositions. One might have a lot of muscle and very little fat and yet come across as overweight by standard height/ weight tables or BMI classifications. On the other hand, the other person might house too much fat yet be deemed as normal/healthy or average weight. This is why body composition, and more specifically fat percentage, is far more important than actual weight.

Fat distribution

Another consideration, apart from just the amount of fat, is the actual distribution of it. In fact, fat distribution is more important than the actual amount when considering health. It is now believed by many health professionals that fat stored mainly around the abdomen (**apple shape**) carries a much higher health risk than fat stored mainly around the hips and thighs (**pear shapes**).

Men tend to accumulate fat around the midsection, between the shoulder blades and close to the internal organs. Women tend to accumulate fat around the hips, thighs, breasts and the triceps-area of the arms. However, after the menopause, women can also accumulate fat around the abdomen, which increases their risk of heart disease as it does for men. Fat distribution partly explains why two very similar people with the same mass and fat percentage can look so different from one another; one might appear slim yet the other overweight.

4.3.1 Measuring body composition

Many people suggest that the simplest way to tell if you are overweight and/or too fat is to just look at yourself in the mirror; others suggest that the best way to tell is based on how you feel. In truth, neither method is advisable. Many people, especially women, perceive themselves as fatter than they actually are, and as discussed above, fat is not spread out the same for every person anyway. Fat distribution is impossible to simply *see*, it might be very high yet appear as very low. There are also those who see themselves as slimmer than they actually are.

How you feel is not a good measure either. If you have never been in particularly good shape (or not for some time), then any improvement will make you feel much better, even when there is ample room and a necessity to continue the improvement. For example, a person who has been 20kg overweight for a long time will feel on top of the world after losing just 5kg of body mass.

Height and weight charts (based on so-called average people) are not the answer either, they are perhaps less useful than the BMI measure.

The most useful information comes from gaining an idea of your fat percentage that will inform you of your body composition. There are several well-known methods for gaining this information; some of these are discussed below.

Dual Energy X-ray Absorptiometry (DEXA)

This is the most accurate method of finding fat percentage, taking over from the hydrostatic weighing method as the gold standard. However, DEXA machines are expensive and require a trained operator so they are normally only found in hospitals and research institutions.

The whole body is X-rayed but the exposure to radiation is well below the level that might cause adverse affects - about a 10th of that used in standard X-rays. The scan measures the density of the body and returns an estimate of lean tissue and fat tissue; an accurate map of how fat is spread throughout your body is provided. The process takes about 10-20 minutes but the results will not normally be available on the same day as the test.

The accuracy of DEXA is often quoted as being at least 98 per cent, but it is still susceptible to operator error, and research has shown different readings among manufacturers. Therefore, it is perhaps best if repeated readings are performed by the same operator and on the same machine - or at least the same manufacturer.

The costs vary quite a lot, but at present a reading is normally about £50-£60 and usually no more than £120. This is quite expensive, so it might be advisable to do your own reading using another device, such as a BIA device (see below), as near to the DEXA scan time (just before or just after) as possible. When you receive your DEXA results you can compare them with your own readings to check the accuracy of your home device.

Hydrostatic weighing (under water)

This is based on Archimedes's principle: 'Any body, wholly or partly immersed in fluid, is buoyed up by a force equal to the weight of the fluid displaced.' A person with more fat-free mass, which primarily includes organs, bone and muscle mass, will weigh more in water than those with less, since lean tissue will sink in water and fat tissue will float. This is because fat density is about 0.9kg per litre and water is about 1.0kg per litre, this is why fat floats in water. Yet muscle is 1.1kg per litre, so it sinks in water. Clearly then, as fat has a larger volume than muscle it takes up more room than muscle of the same mass. Hydrostatic weighing was the most accurate method of finding a person's fat percentage for some time before being replaced by the new gold standard, DEXA.

The subject is weighed on dry land and then, after exhaling as much air as possible, lowered into water whilst sitting on a special chair and weighed again under water. The subject is completely immersed for 10-15 seconds and since the process is often repeated as many as 10 times it can take about 45-60 minutes to complete. A computer will estimate the person's fat percentage after several adjustments are made, such as for water density and temperature and consideration for air left in the lungs.

This method requires special equipment and is usually only found in universities and hospitals, but the current price is reasonable at £10-£40, especially since it has an accuracy of about 97-98 per cent. However, it seems to slightly underestimate the fat mass of athletes as they tend to have denser muscles and bones than non-athletes.

Skin-fold callipers

These are used to measure layers of fat underneath the skin at various parts of the body; triceps, biceps, hip bone area, lower back, abdomen, thigh, and under the shoulder blade. These measurements are then used as parameters in other equations that account for age, gender, hidden fat (around the organs), and other things.

This method is as accurate as the person taking the measurements, and does not take into consideration that fat distribution is not predictable and that much fat is intra-abdominal. That said, there are different equations; some are more accurate for the average population and others are more accurate for lean and athletic people.

The accuracy levels are said to be in the range of 94-96 per cent, but many experts put the figure a bit lower since this method is largely dependent on the skill of the user, and there is no general way of knowing this.

Bioelectrical Impedance Analysis (BIA)

BIA devices are normally available as either handheld equipment or the usual bath-room - step on - scales; some include both. They work by measuring the current flow between two electrodes. For the handheld versions these electrodes are normally placed between both hands, or one hand and the opposite foot. The stand-on scales have the electrodes as part of the surface of the scales, where you place each foot. A weak current is sent through the body which is met by resistance, depending primarily on muscle mass, fat and hydration. A slower signal implies more fat and a faster signal implies less fat. The resistance measured is substituted into an equation that usually considers height, body mass, gender, hydration and age.

Readings tend to be lower soon after bathing or exercise, and higher soon after waking or consumption. In view of this, the general advice is to avoid consumption for four hours and exercise for twelve hours, before testing.

The accuracy of such scales has improved a lot since they first became readily available in the mid-80s, and the equations have been improved upon over the years, but more work needs to be done. The step-on scales send the current through the legs and trunk, so fat in other areas is not contributing to the resistance. This means that if the fat is much higher in the mid-section than other areas, the overall fat percentage will be too high, and if it is much lower in the mid-section, the scale will read too low. Similarly for the hand-held devices, which measure between the arms and upper body. This seems to imply that the best BIA scales are those that send the current between hand and foot, but this is not necessarily the case. Nonetheless, BIA devices are good value for money, even though they seem to overestimate the fat percentage of lean people by 2-5 per cent and underestimate the fat percentage of overweight people by the same range.

The Bod Pod

The Bod Pod is a computerised, egg-shaped, chamber which accurately assesses fat mass and the location of fat stores. It uses the patented Air Displacement Plethysmography method - similar to Archimedes' principle used by DEXA - which considers the volume and mass inside the chamber when it is empty, and again when the subject is inside. The results are used to calculate the fat mass percentage.

It compares well to the DEXA method for accuracy, and is also far quicker at only 10 minutes in total, and much cheaper. It seems that the Bod Pod will soon be the new gold standard for measuring fat percentage.

Near Infrared Interactance (NIR)

Near Infrared Interactance uses an infrared beam that is shone through the upper arm, then reflected, off the bone, to the analyser. The amount of light reflected corresponds to the amount of fat there, and this is the main problem; it makes an assumption that the amount of fat in the upper arm corresponds to the body's total fat proportion.

In its favour, it does take into consideration the person's age, gender, height, mass and activity levels, but this does not compensate for its lack of regard for the spread of fat. At best though, it can still give an accuracy level of about 95%, perhaps in those who do not have an accumulated area of fat, or those that do not have a high fat percentage anyway. At worst it may only be 90% accurate, so for these reasons it is generally not recommended.

Fat percentage and true fat loss

Percentages are often the cause of misleading or misunderstood information, so it is good to know that a small reduction in overall fat percentage is actually higher than it might seem. Unfortunately, a small increase in overall fat percentage is also higher than it might appear. Devices that measure body composition give the overall fat percentage, but what is equally interesting is the actual amount of fat (in kg) to which this percentage corresponds. The calculation is simple:

Expressing body fat percentage in kg

BM × fat percentage figure = amount of body fat in kg

Example

To keep the figures and calculations simple, let's consider an athlete who has a body mass of 50kg, of which 10 per cent is fat. Therefore:

BM × fat percentage = amount of body fat in kg = 50 × 0.10 = 5
So of the 50kg of BM the amount in fat is 5kg.

Such information is useful when the 'true' fat loss percentage is desired; the method is as follows:

Method to find true fat loss percentage

1. Note your previous amount of body fat in kg.

2. Find your current amount of body fat in kg.

3.Subtract the figure from step 2 from the figure at step 1.

Note: if your fat has increased, this figure will be negative.

4. Divide the answer obtained at step 3 by the figure from step 1.

5. Express the answer obtained at step 4 by multiplying by 100.

Example

Let's assume that the same athlete, after some weeks of intensive exercise, has remained at 50kg but her overall fat percentage dropped to 9 per cent.

1. Previous body fat accounts for 5kg of BM

2. Current body fat accounts for 4.5kg of BM (since 9 per cent of 50 is 4.5)

3. 5kg - 4.5kg = 0.5kg

4. (0.5kg)/(5kg) = 0.1

5. 0.1 × 100 = 10

So this athlete reduced her fat by 10 per cent, not one per cent, as it may have appeared.

Percentages cause further confusion when fluids (among other things) are consumed or excreted. For example, consider a athlete that has a BM of 56kg, of which 20 per cent is fat; in other words, 11.2kg of her BM is fat. Now let's suppose that she (unwisely) guzzles down a litre of water, this will increase her BM by about 1kg, so she now as a BM of 57kg. What is interesting is how this action affects her fat percentage; her actual amount of fat will stay the same (as water does not include fat or any other form of energy), yet the increase in BM will affect the overall fat percentage.

In this example, our athlete has gone from 56kg and 20 per cent fat to 57kg and about 19.6 per cent fat - i.e., increasing her BM by consuming fluids actually lowered her fat percentage. The calculations are not important, but it is useful to be aware that fluctuations in BM and fat percentage occur throughout the day for a variety of reasons.

Fat loss/weight loss predictions

There are many questions posed with regards to predicting fat loss and weight loss, especially by those new to training or those interested in losing fat. Some example questions are:

1. What would my body mass be if I lost *x* per cent fat?
2. If I lost *x*kg, what would my fat percentage go down to?
3. How much fat per cent do I lose for each kg that I drop in body mass?

Such questions are difficult to answer accurately, but an idea can be obtained by experimenting with the corresponding Excel programme.

Fat distribution tests without machines

The following two tests should not be regarded as an alternative to knowing your fat percentage, but rather as necessary additional information regarding the spread of fat around the midsection - the area of most concern.

The waist/hip ratio is a common test that gives a good estimate regarding abdominal fat and its implications. For instance, a person with a waist/hip ratio of 1.1 has at least double the chance of suffering a heart attack than someone whose ratio is less than 0.95. However, for a more informative reading of your ratio, see figure **4.10**, below.

Waist-to-hip ratio (general)*

- **men**: waist measurement divided by hip measurement should be less than or equal to 0.95.
- **women**: waist measurement divided by hip measurement should be less than or equal to 0.85.

*It is irrelevant what measures you use for this test, so long as you are consistent.

Figure 4.10 Waist-to-hip ratio categories

Gender	Acceptable ratio, x			Unacceptable ratio, x	
	Excellent	Good	Average	High	Extreme
Male	$x < 0.85$	$0.85 \leq x \leq 0.90$	$0.90 < x \leq 0.95$	$0.95 < x \leq 1.00$	$x > 1.00$
Female	$x < 0.75$	$0.75 \leq x \leq 0.80$	$0.80 < x \leq 0.85$	$0.85 < x \leq 0.90$	$x > 0.90$

Bear in mind that if someone were underweight, then both the hips and the waist would decrease at the same time, perhaps proportionally. This means that these tests could show good/excellent abdominal fat levels, when in fact the person has too little fat. This can work in the other extreme too. If both the waist and hips were too high, the reading could easily be misleading. For example, if a man had a waist and hip size of 92cm and 100cm, respectively, then the waist-to-hip ratio would return an acceptable-average result, even though both these measurements are probably too high.

The waist circumference method below is an even simpler test that has shown to be a good estimation of excessive intra-abdominal fat.

Waist circumference:

- **men**: waist measurement greater than or equal to 94cm implies excessive abdominal fat
- **women**: waist measurement greater than or equal to 80cm implies excessive abdominal fat

4.3.2 Health and performance

Excess fat will hinder performance in most activities relevant to training, and is a major contributor to health problems. Fat imbalance will cause performance problems with respect to:

- strength
- speed
- endurance
- oxygen intake
- fatigue
- power

Too much fat is useless extra weight; you are carrying extra weight that serves no purpose, and all it will do is slow you down. There seems to be no performance loss due to very low fat percentages, but there are many health concerns to consider. Fat imbalance will cause health problems with respect to your:

- general mobility
- joints (especially your back, knees and ankles)
- heart
- lung capacity
- bones
- testosterone

With regards to fitness, there is at least a two-fold problem when carrying too much fat. When carrying excess fat you are forced to train with extra weight, yet you have less muscle strength to cope with this extra weight. This means your back (lower back in particular) and other joints have to take far more stress than they are designed for.

4.4 Fat in food

There are three types of fat in food, differing from one another according to their molecular structure. However, they are often put into one of only two groups:

- **non-essential fats** - saturated and monounsaturated fats
- **essential fats** - polyunsaturated fats

However, it is also common (perhaps more so) to consider them as:

- saturated fat
- unsaturated fat - monounsaturated and polyunsaturated fats

Saturated fatty acids

Saturates can increase low-density lipoprotein (LDL), bad cholesterol, which increases the risk of heart disease. It is generally recommended to limit its intake to 10 per cent of total calorie intake, but less is perhaps better. Some say none at all is best but others suggest a minimum requirement as none may increase the risk of strokes and certain types of haemorrhage. However, it seems that no lower limit is generally agreed upon at present. Saturates are not considered as essential nutrients, but they are stored fats so they can be used as energy. They are usually from animal sources and are found in butter, hard margarine, cheese, milk (whole milk in particular), and foods that contain such ingredients, such as milk chocolate, biscuits, and pies. Saturates are clearly visible as the white fat in meat and under the skin of poultry. Saturates are normally solid at room temperature.

Monounsaturated

As for saturated fats, monounsaturates are also often considered as non-essential nutrients, but they are also stored fats so they too can be used as energy. However, unlike saturated fats, monounsaturated fat can reduce total cholesterol, in particular LDL cholesterol, without affecting the beneficial cholesterol, HDL. Some books refer to omega-9, a monounsaturated fat, as a semi-essential fatty acid, as the body can only produce it if there is enough omega-3 and omega-6 present. If not, it becomes essential, as it will need to be obtained via the diet.

The highest source of omega-9 comes from olive oil, but monounsaturates in general are also found in avocados, oats, various nuts, and specifically in several nut and seed oils such as peanut oil and sesame oil. Monounsaturated fat is normally liquid at room temperature.

Polyunsaturated

Polyunsaturated fats are considered as essential fats because they cannot be produced in the body (you must supply them in your diet), and the body needs them. Polyunsaturated fats can reduce LDL blood levels, but they can also reduce the good cholesterol slightly. Hence why some advise an intake of monounsaturated fats if you consume high amounts of polyunsaturated fats; in theory this will offset the reduction of good cholesterol.

The body can make all the fatty acids it needs except two, omega-3 and omega-6. They are a sub-category of polyunsaturated fats that cannot be made in the body; *they* are the **essential fatty acids**. Omega-3 and omega-6 fatty acids can be further divided, according to their molecular structure, into two groups, as shown blow.

- **omega-3** family, derived from alpha-linolenic acid (ALA)
  Eicosapentanoic acid (**EPA**)
  Docosahexanoic acid (**DHA**)
- **omega-6** family, derived from linoleic acid (LA)
  Gamma-linoleic acid (**GLA**)
  Docosapentanoic acid (**DPA**).

EPA and DHA are converted into other substances that control many key functions, such as:

- prevention of blood clotting
- inflammation regulation
- widening and constriction of blood vessels
- the immune system

Studies have shown that those with the highest intake of omega-3 have a lower risk of heart attacks. The best sources of EPA and DHA are oily fish: mackerel, and especially sardines and salmon, are all very high in EPA and DHA. Other good sources are linseeds (also called flaxseed), pumpkin seeds, walnuts, soya beans and dark green leafy vegetables.

GLA acid DPA are very important for:

- healthy functioning of cell membranes
- healthy skin

Those on low fat diets are often deficient in omega-6 and this is often obvious by their poor skin condition - usually very dry and flaky. Most people in the UK have a greater intake of omega-6 than omega-3. The right balance, though, is very important, since they both compete for the same enzymes to metabolise them.

Recommended intakes for fat are unclear even for general nutrition, let alone for sports nutrition. Certainly most agree that over 35 per cent of your daily calorie intake is too much, and that too little is not healthy either. However, some say that a little saturates are necessary, yet others regard them as entirely unnecessary. There is also disagreement as to the ratio in which monounsaturates and polyunsaturates should be consumed, and unlike protein and carbohydrates, there is little or no suggestion for grammes of fat per kilogramme of body mass, apart from those on fat-loss diets (*see* **5.3, Food and fat loss**); nearly all suggestions come in the less useful form, *percentage of total calorie intake*. Nonetheless, a suggested intake is provided below that allows room for the required intakes of protein and carbohydrates of sports people, and also a little flexibility for saturates.

- total intake: 20 per cent
- essential fatty acids: 7 per cent (3.5% of omega-3 and 3.5% of omega-6)
- monounsaturated fat: 7 per cent
- saturated fats: less than 10 per cent (or consume more essential and mono-unsaturated fat)

Though this guide suggests a total intake of 20 per cent, this may be increased to about 25 per cent - or perhaps more, depending on the individual's particular needs. Once the necessary carbohydrate and protein levels are met, the rest can be made up from more carbohydrates or good fat, depending on requirements or preferences. Incidentally, more protein to make up calorific needs is generally not recommended (*see* **3.3.2**).

4.4.1 Omega-3 and performance

Some studies have shown that omega-3 fatty acids may improve athletic performance in both aerobic and anaerobic exercise, but other papers dispute this. Some of the claimed benefits are:

- improved oxygen delivery
- enhanced aerobic metabolism
- increased energy levels and stamina
- increased training intensity and duration
- improved recovery time
- reduced inflammation

Regardless of benefits to sports performance, none show an unfavourable effect and in any case, omega-3 has many well documented health benefits.

4.4.2 Trans-fatty acids

These are also known as hydrogenated fats, which are used in abundance in many foods such as, cakes, biscuits, margarines and low-fat spreads. Among other things, they are thought to lower HDL and raise LDL - in other words, lower the good cholesterol and raise the bad cholesterol. They should really be avoided completely, but the Department of Health (DoH) recommends a maximum of 5g a day; perhaps this is more realistic than complete avoidance. As an alternative to margarine and butter, you could try pumpkin seed butter; it has no trans-fatty acids, but plenty of good cholesterol.

5 Losing the Fat

This chapter begins with a detailed account of the metabolic rate, and includes a clear explanation of some of its aspects that people find confusing. This is followed by a brief look at dietary-induced thermogenesis (DIT) and some of its misconceptions. Food and its relation to fat loss, such as the so-called fat-burning foods, are also briefly, but succinctly, addressed before moving on to the all-important total daily energy expenditure (TDEE); essential for athletes to fine-tune their intakes. Various fat loss methods are then discussed and each is coupled with a clearly worked example. A close look at two common food guides is given, the food-triangle and the food-plate (including its easily overlooked problems of accuracy), before the chapter closes with a detailed discussion on fat cells.

5.1 Resting Metabolic Rate (RMR)

The RMR refers to the amount of kcal that you would burn if you did nothing all day, if you literally remained in bed (awake) for 24 hours. It is the essential energy required just for you to function, and accounts for 60-75% of your total daily energy expenditure.

The **Basal Metabolic Rate** (**BMR**) is commonly misunderstood to be the same as the RMR, but strictly speaking it is not. The BMR is the energy expended whilst in a post-absorptive state, i.e. the digestive system is inactive, so it requires about 12 hours of fasting. The RMR is a less restrictive and a more common measurement of metabolic rate.

Calculating your RMR

There are several ways to calculate the RMR, some more accurate and relevant than others, but the Mifflin-St Jeor method was chosen as the standard throughout this book as it seems to be the one most commonly used by sport scientists (*see Equation 5.1, below*). However, for the sake of interest, two further well-known methods can be found in *Appendix A*. It might be a good idea to check your RMR (and perhaps that of others) using all three methods, as this should give you a good idea of the range of RMR values, depending on the method used. The original equation used to estimate the BMR, the Harris-Benedict method, was published in 1918, yet the modern alternatives are barely a few per cent more accurate.

Equation 5.1 Standard RMR calculations (Mifflin-St Jeor)

Male	10(BM) + (6.25H) - (5A) + 5 = RMR kcal/day
Female	(10BM) + (6.25H) - (5A) - 161 = RMR kcal/day

Where:

BM is body mass in kg, H is height in cm and A is age in years

Example 5.1 RMR calculation

A 35-year old woman with a body mass of 53kg and height of 162cm would have the following RMR:

$$(10BM) + (6.25H) - (5A) - 161 = RMR$$
$$10 \times 53 + 6.25 \times 162 - 5 \times 35 - 161 = 1206.5$$

Hence, her RMR is about 1207kcal a day, according to the Mifflin-St Jeor RMR method.

There are also a number of factors that will increase or decrease a person's metabolic rate, not all of which are factored into the standard method:

1. **Body composition**: the more muscle tissue we have, the faster the RMR; the more fat we have, the slower it becomes.
2. **Age**: as we age, there is a tendency to gain more fat than muscle, and this is part of the reason why our metabolism slows down.
3. **Height**: tall people have a higher RMR in general; a larger frame requires more calories to be burned just for maintenance.
4. **Ambient temperature**: we need to burn energy to cool down, but also to warm up.
5. **Fasting**: when we fast our body reacts by going into so-called *starvation mode*. The body will need to be more fuel-efficient, so our RMR slows down.

6. **Thyroxine**: this is the thyroid hormone that regulates the body's RMR; if more is produced the RMR becomes faster, if less is produced the RMR becomes slower.

7. **Fever**: this is defined as a raised body temperature. As a result, our RMR increases to help fight the illness and also to cool the body.

8. **Stress**: stress releases a fat-storing hormone called cortisol, and can therefore increase the RMR.

9. **Ethnicity/individuality**: it is possible that the RMR calculation method used as standard in this text may not be suitable for certain groups of people or individuals.

Some sources include activity levels within the RMR calculation, since exercising can affect your resting metabolism. In this book, any activity (training, work, housework etc.) is not included in the RMR calculation (*see 5.4 for their inclusion*).

⚠ Misconception about body composition and RMR

Research has consistently shown that as total body mass increases, so does the RMR because a larger frame requires more calories burned just for basic maintenance. However, this point is often misunderstood, since it appears to conflict with item one above, which states, '…the more fat we have the slower it (RMR) becomes'. A common question is: 'How can an overweight person have a faster RMR if fat is supposed to make it slow down?' This question will be easier to answer using an example. Consider the four potential situations for the same athlete given in the table below.

	Various considerations of the *same* Male Athlete			
	A	**B**	**C**	**D**
BMI classification	Normal	Normal	Overweight because of too much fat	Overweight because of heavy muscle
Body mass	70kg (say) Normal mass		85kg (say) Above normal mass	
Fat percentage	Normal	Too high	Much too high (poor)	Low (healthy)
RMR	Normal	Slower than average	Faster than average	Fastest of all

These results tell us that:

- **Column A**: when this athlete has a normal BMI, BM and fat percentage, his RMR will also be normal; as would be expected.
- **Column B:** when this athlete has a normal BMI, but a high level of fat, his RMR is slower than average because fat slows down the metabolism.
- **Column C:** when this athlete is overweight according to his BMI and also has a very high fat level, his RMR may be faster than average, since the demands of a larger frame can (but not necessarily) offset the slowing effect of fat.
- **Column D:** when this athlete is overweight according to his BMI, but his fat levels are low-healthy, his RMR will be fastest of all, since lean muscle speeds up the metabolism.

As you can see, there are many considerations regarding the metabolism, and none is more important than another.

5.1.1 Training and your RMR

Resistance training has consistently shown to increase the RMR, and this makes sense since the more lean muscle tissue a person possesses the faster the RMR. Many sources suggest that an increase of just 0.5kg of muscle will burn another 30-50kcal a day (some suggest a lot more) - an extra 210-350kcal a week, when you are at rest! However, these figures are largely unfounded. Even though it is true that muscle burns three times as many calories as fat, the actual number of calories burned owing to muscle increase is a lot more modest.

- fat burns about 4.5kcal a kg
- muscle burns about 13.5kcal a kg

Certainly, if you lose 0.5kg of fat, but maintain your BM by increasing your muscle mass by 0.5kg, that is a 1kg improvement to your body composition. However, as far as your RMR is concerned, this means an increase of only about 9kcal a day - 13.5kcal from a 1kg muscle increase, minus 4.5kcal from a 1kg fat decrease. To keep the figures simple though:

- Every 1kg of muscle gained, whilst also losing 1kg of fat, means a daily RMR increase of about 10kcal.

Your metabolic rate remains higher after exercise, since your body needs to burn energy to pay off the oxygen debt and also to cool down. How much depends on duration, intensity, type and so on. This post-exercise increase in RMR is often called the **after burn**, the energy that is obtained mainly from the body's fat stores. Both resistance and aerobic training are important when on a fat-loss programme, or perhaps most programmes for that matter. However, many studies have also shown that those on a combination of anaerobic and aerobic exercise have better results than those on anaerobic or aerobic programmes alone. Whilst most of the recent papers seem to use a combination of anaerobic and aerobic training on alternating days, there are other methods of combining the two. It might be worth experimenting by mixing them within the same training period. The question is, though: which way round is better, anaerobic followed by aerobic, or aerobic followed by anaerobic? Theoretically, both methods make sense, but both also have potential drawbacks. Anaerobic exercise first - and for long enough - will deplete the glycogen stores, and may therefore force the body to burn even more fat than usual to fuel the ensuing aerobic exercise. However, this method might mean less energy is available for the aerobic exercise, which overall might mean less fat burning because you will be unable to continue exercising as long. Doing it the other way round - i.e., aerobic followed by anaerobic, may cause a similar problem. A lot more research needs to be done before any 'best' method is known, assuming there is one. It should come as no surprise if it is found to be an individualistic matter rather than a best-method-for-all. Apart from all the usual variables such as gender, ethnicity and mass, it may turn out that the ratio of fast twitch to slow twitch muscle has an important part to play.

Research has shown that those on aerobics-only programmes do lose significant amounts of fat, but they also tend to lose a little muscle as well. A little muscle loss is not unexpected or damaging, especially for those on fat loss programmes specifically. However, those on anaerobic-aerobic combined programmes tended to lose even more fat than those on aerobic-only programmes whilst also gaining muscle.

High-intensity interval training (HIIT)

Despite the well documented benefits of anaerobic-aerobic combined training methods, the last 15 years or so have consistently and increasingly shown the HIIT method to be the best training method to lose fat. HIIT, also called **high-intensity intermittent exercise (HIIE)**, is a training method that includes bursts of high intensity exercise followed by low to moderate - recovery time - exercise. The original method constituted a high-intensity exercise immediately followed by a medium-intensity exercise in a 2:1 ratio. For example, this might be 30 seconds of high-intensity boxing pad work followed by the same activity (though not necessarily) for 15 seconds of low-medium intensity; typically, HIIT lasts only for 10 to 20 minutes, yet the results are remarkable. There are now several variations of HIIT, but the principals are the same. There are three very encouraging advantages with this method of training:

1. The time required is considerably lower than that of a typical anaerobic or aerobic programme.
2. HIIT significantly improves both the aerobic and anaerobic capacity.
3. Most sports are HIIT by nature: football, boxing, tennis, squash and so on.

Item **3.** above should be of particular interest to those needing to lose fat, or for those just interested in improving their health and fitness. Motivating oneself to train at home with the latest Internet shopping fad (and soon-to-be dust collector) will inevitably become more and more difficult. If you do not look forward to your training, why would you keep to it? Whereas, joining a sports club and participating in an activity you really enjoy will make it a hobby, in which case you are far more likely to keep with it, and you will be training without even thinking about it.

5.2 Energy and fat loss

This section briefly discusses the idea of energy balance, followed by the basics of dietary-induced thermogenesis, the energy burned to digest food, and a few words on the misconceptions about thermogenesis and water.

5.2.1 Energy balance

A balanced energy intake is such that the exact number of calories consumed is the same as those expended. In reality this is impossible, since we never intake and expend exactly same amount of energy in any one day. So although there is always an imbalance, it is quite easy to make this imbalance insignificant, i.e. an imbalance that will not make a noticeable effect on our body mass.

Energy intake that is near enough the same as energy expenditure is referred to as a *balanced energy intake*; in theory, it is the intake required to maintain your body mass. A *positive energy intake* is an intake that is significantly more than you burn; enough to cause an increase in body mass. A *negative energy intake* is an intake that is significantly less than you burn; enough to cause a reduction in body mass. Thus, a negative energy intake is the answer for weight loss, but this may not necessarily mean fat loss, and in any case, there are many other considerations.

5.2.2 Thermogenesis

Thermogenesis is a process of heat production in organisms. However, the term 'thermogenesis' is often incorrectly thought of as necessarily meaning 'dietary-induced thermogenesis', or the thermic effect. In fact, there are three main types of thermogenesis concerned with the human body:

- exercise heat
- thermo-regulatory (keeping the body temperature regulated, sometimes via shivering)
- dietary-induced thermogenesis (DIT).

Dietary-induced thermogenesis (DIT)

When you eat, your body temperature changes a little, and a change in heat means energy is being burned. So the very act of eating or drinking actually burns some calories. The macronutrients and alcohol each have a different thermal effect, but depend on the balance of each:

- **protein:** consuming it burns off about 20-35% of its own calories
- **carbohydrates:** consuming it burns off 5-15% of its own calories
- **fat*:** consuming it burns off up to about 3% of its own calories
- **alcohol*:** consuming it burns off about 8% of its own calories

*The thermic effect of fat is one of much debate; some papers even suggest that fat has the same thermic effect as carbohydrates. There also seems to be much disagreement about the DIT of alcohol; some put it as high as protein.

It must be noted that the DIT percentage given above are general. Results come from a variety of test conditions, including different diets, results attained from static and/or dynamic subjects, obese subjects, normal or fit subjects, sometimes single genders, and subjects with certain medical conditions. Nevertheless, it seems that a diet low in protein and carbohydrates will mean that the body will produce less heat, and therefore burn fewer calories. However, in practice, the diet will be a mixture of all the macronutrients, and perhaps alcohol as well.

DIT is just a point of interest for our purposes; it makes no significant difference to the overall calorie intake, and has no bearing on performance. Many experts suggest an estimated DIT of 5-15% if alcohol is part of your usual intake, or about 10% if it is not. Thus, a 2,500 kcal diet, that excludes alcohol, only burns about 250 kcal through DIT. This is not nearly enough to be the sole consideration for either weight loss or weight gain.

Thermogenesis and water

There is much information on the Internet about the **negative calories** of iced water; the calculation being that every litre of water (which has no calories) requires about 30-40kcal to bring it to body temperature. In fact, DIT will occur with all foods and drinks, hot or cold; so the only requirement to attain a negative calorie intake is for the energy necessary for DIT to be greater than the calorie total of the food or drink consumed. These includes very low calorie foods such as celery, green leafy vegetables, cabbage and certain fruits, and drinks with few or no calories, such as teas, black coffee and water.

In truth, the thermogenic reaction to water, including iced and distilled water, has been shown to be even lower than the (already insignificant) theoretical 30-40kcal mentioned above. Using the idea of negative calories to reduce fat is a complete waste of time, and may even be harmful. Eating low calorie food, ice-cubes or drinking several litres of water will not provide vital nutrients. Too much fluid may even flush out many nutrients before they have been absorbed and may also overtax the kidneys, leading to other problems.

5.3 Food and fat loss

There is currently much talk about so-called fat-burning foods; such foods are said to burn more fat than others by speeding up the metabolism. Whilst it is true that certain foods cause a greater metabolic rate than others, the claims are often unfounded at worst and misleading at best. A simple Internet search will soon direct you to a long list of such foods from apples to watermelons, and those of almost every letter of the alphabet in between. Most of these foods have not been thoroughly tested, or even at all, and many that have did not show a significant metabolic effect. Moreover, foods found in such lists are generally wholesome anyway, and should therefore be part of your general intake regardless.

The more common foods that have been well-tested and do seem to have genuine fat-burning claims are caffeine, ephedrine (a chemical found in some evergreen shrubs, though normally taken as a supplement), capsaicin (a chemical found in capsicums, including sweet peppers and chilli peppers), and green tea. There is evidence of an increased energy expenditure of 4 to 5 per cent and a significant increase of fat oxidation by 10-16 per cent. However, much or most of the research appears to be based on obese subjects that were put on very low calorie diets, in which the main interest was weight loss, not enhanced performances in sports and exercise.

If you do choose to include more of these foods in your diet it is advisable to take the natural form; the supplement forms, which will be discussed in *Chapter 8*, often have unpleasant side effects.

Carbohydrates

Any excess carbohydrates consumed should be converted into glycogen, provided there is enough storage space available, and provided there is only a low-to-modest rise in blood glucose; meaning, you should be consuming low-to-moderate GL foods. Meals that are rich in carbohydrates curb the appetite for one to three hours after consumption, this perhaps corresponds to periods during which the insulin has been raised. A fast rise in blood glucose (via high GL foods) causes a rapid release of insulin and this may result in the insulin turning the excess carbohydrates into fat, then depositing them into your fat cells. However, it now seems clear that in most cases very little carbohydrate is actually converted and stored as fat, since the body is thought to auto-regulate to match the intake of glucose.

Protein

When excessive protein is eaten, the amino part of the molecule is excreted via the urine, assuming there is enough water available to dilute it; otherwise it could become toxic. The rest of the molecule is either used directly for energy or stored; if there is room it will be stored as glycogen, otherwise it will be stored as fat. However, as for glucose, this is not common, since the body is also thought to auto-regulate to match its intake of amino acids.

Leptin is a protein hormone discovered in 1994, though its effects were first observed some decades before. It is produced by fat cells in the body and released into the bloodstream in proportion to the amount of energy stored in fat. It acts as a signal to the brain to inform of satiety, thus helping to regulate energy intake and energy expenditure; however, some people are genetically less responsive to leptin than others. Although it reduces the physiological need and desire to eat, it has no bearing on the sensory signals (especially smell and sight) that stimulate hunger, such as sweet cravings. In any case, some may choose to ignore their feelings of fullness.

Levels of leptin in the blood vary on a 24-hour cycle; high levels tend to be present after eating and low levels during fasting. Since leptin acts to curb the appetite and increase the metabolism, it may seem that higher levels are more beneficial for weight loss, but high leptin levels in your blood eventually result in leptin insensitivity - similar to a diabetic's response to insulin. Moreover, they are made in the fat cells, so higher levels of leptin would actually mean more fat. In contrast, low levels seem to promote a feeling of hunger by increasing the sensitivity of response to a hormone in the gut that reduces the feelings of hunger. Therefore, a low level of leptin with a higher sensitivity to them is supportive of a timely satiety and the maintenance of a high metabolism; both of which are essential for weight regulation.

The body has to make its own leptin and it cannot be absorbed by the digestive tract anyway, so a food source rich in leptin is not the answer. However, certain foods seem to make the body more sensitive to leptin (the reasons are still unclear) such as kidney beans, lentils and some vegetables, but particularly fish.

Although this chapter is dedicated to losing fat it should be noted that leptin helps in weight regulation, which therefore includes weight gain as well as weight loss. Many people, especially female athletes and those with certain eating disorders, have too little fat and are therefore in need of higher leptin levels for weight regulation. Whilst it has not proved possible to use leptin as a drug to contain the appetite, it can be administered to help those in need of increased levels

Fat

Unlike glucose and amino acids, fat does not produce a rise in blood sugar that will reduce the appetite, and neither does it increase your desire to burn off energy. So it seems that fat does not auto-regulate, which is perhaps owing to the large storage capacity for it in the body. Fat is digested and absorbed a lot more slowly, and can even depress blood glucose, so the appetite is less satisfied and you have no *burst of energy* feeling either. Fat is far higher in calories than protein and carbohydrates, and has a low bulk; hence why it tends to make people overeat quite easily.

Alcohol

Alcohol has a high calorie value and is easily over-consumed. Furthermore, alcohol cannot be stored in the body; it must be oxidised and converted into energy. However, while this is happening the oxidation of fat and carbohydrates is suppressed, so this means that if the glycogen storage has peaked it will be stored as fat. In addition to this, alcoholic drinks often have a very high sugar content, which further increases the calories and consequently the chances of excessive calories being stored as fat.

5.4 Total energy expenditure

For part of these calculations we will need an idea of the amount of calories burned during particular exercises. The table in *Fig 5.1*, below, is based on an athlete weighing about 65kg; a heavier athlete will burn more calories, and a lighter athlete will burn less. So for every 10kg above or below 65kg, you should add or subtract five to 10 per cent accordingly. There is also a difference according to such things as age, gender and fitness levels.

The problem is that one source of **training calorie estimates** will rarely agree with another; the differences can be vast! So even if you find a table that appears to cater for you, it does not necessarily mean that it will be more accurate; it is no exaggeration to say that you could easily add or subtract 100-200kcal to each activity listed below.

Total daily energy expenditure (TDEE)

This is the estimated total of all calories burned in a day. There are several ways to find this total estimate, but this book contains the information on just two methods. The standard method for this book is presented below and the other can be found at the lower part of appendix A.

TDEE calculation method

The TDEE calculation consists of the four main steps:

1. calculate your RMR
2. multiply your RMR by activity factor
3. calculate your average exercise-energy expenditure
4. sum the values obtained from 2 and 3 above

Fig 5.1 Training calories for 65kg athlete

Activity type	Intensity level	Kilocalories burned an hour
Aerobics	Low - high	400 - 520
Cycling	Low	250
Cycling	Medium	385
Jogging	Low	550
Jogging	Medium	680
Sparring (boxing only)	Low	600
Sparring (boxing only)	Medium	865
Sparring (all strikes)	Low	700
Sparring (all strikes)	Medium	850
Sparring (grappling)	Medium	700
Sparring (MMA)	Low	700
Sparring (MMA)	Medium	850
Walking	Low-medium	150 - 250
Walking	High	280
Weight/resistance training	Medium-high	270 - 450

Step 1

Calculate your RMR *(see section 5.1)*.

Step 2

Multiply your RMR by your normal, daily activity factor:

sedentary: RMR × 1.4
moderately active: RMR × 1.7
very active: RMR × 2.0

Sedentary includes sitting or standing activities such as, driving, cooking, painting, ironing, sewing, watching TV and *writing books such as this*. **Moderately active** includes regular walking, housework, gardening, and general maintenance work. **Very active** includes manual digging, heavy warehouse work, furniture removal and labouring. These estimates are not always easy to use as it is often difficult to choose among sedentary, moderate, and very active, and in reality a multiple other than 1.4, 1.7 or 2.0 would be more accurate.

Step 3

Calculate your average daily calories burned from exercise by referring to *Fig 5.1* above, or a book or Internet site specific to your sport. Since most people do not train every day (not advisable anyway), the daily energy expenditure from exercise is an average - in other words, the total weekly exercise kcal divided by seven. However, some require or prefer a slightly more accurate measure, so they calculate the energy burned on training and non-training days separately.

Step 4

Finally, sum the total of *Steps 2* and *3*; this gives your estimated TDEE. Meeting this total should, in theory, maintain your current body mass; hence why your TDEE is also referred to as your **weight maintenance intake**. The other method, described in *Appendix A,* does not separate normal daily activities and exercise. It uses a multiple that considers both combined, but it has more multiples to choose from, and also uses different multiples for males and females. It is a good idea to experiment with both methods so that you can observe the differences.

Example 5.4 Total daily energy expenditure (TDEE) calculation

Assume that a 65kg athlete has an RMR of 1726, is moderately active, and engages in high-intensity aerobics four times a week:

1. RMR = 1726 (given)
2. Moderately active means: RMR × 1.4 = 2416
3. High-intensity aerobics for 40 minutes burns about 347kcal according to the table in *Fig 5.1* (from: 520 multiplied by 2/3, since 40 min is two thirds of an hour). At four times a week this gives a total of 4 × 347 = 1388kcal or an average of 1388/7 = 198kcal a day.
4. So the (average) TDEE for this athlete is (2416 + 198) = 2614kcal.

5.5 Fat loss methods

There seems to be two main methods for losing fat: reducing the daily calorie intake by a fixed amount (normally between 500 and 1000kcal) or reducing the daily calorie intake by a fixed percentage (normally between 15 and 20 per cent). Unfortunately, neither of these guarantees the consumption of the minimum requirements of macronutrients, but before looking at these methods it is important to keep some general points in mind.

Regardless of your intentions, **fat intake should not exceed 50 per cent of your total calories, but should generally be between 15 and 30 per cent, which often works out to about 0.5-1.0g/kg/BM.** Moreover, of your total fat intake, a **minimum of 14 per cent should come from unsaturated fats**, but your saturated fats should be less than 10 per cent. A maximum fat intake of 50 per cent might seem excessive, but it may be necessary for some athletes, such as those involved in regular high-volume training or events in very cold conditions for long periods.

Carbohydrates should continue to be about 50 to 70 per cent of your total calorie intake, but it is more important to consider your minimum daily energy requirements. If you are in training, it is especially important to consume your minimum amount of energy from carbohydrates (*Chapter 2: Carbohydrates*) and in some cases protein as well (*Chapter 3: Protein*).

A lack of energy provided, in particular carbohydrates, will mean you cannot train as effectively because you will not have enough energy. This means you will burn fewer calories and therefore less fat. So **it is vital to consume your minimum carbohydrate intake**, even when on a weight-loss programme. A higher-than-normal intake of protein is also worth considering as it can offset some of the lean tissue loss, and has the additional benefit of increasing satiety. **For weight loss, the recommend intake is about 1.6g per kg of body mass** (*see 3.2*).

If you reduce your normal energy intake too much it will cause the body to slow down your metabolic rate in an effort to reserve energy; this will also cause protein oxidisation and glycogen depletion. The end result will mean a lack of energy, loss of lean muscle, and an uncomfortable feeling of hunger. The more you reduce your normal energy intake, the worse these effects will become. In short, the body reacts well to a small deficit from your usual energy intake by burning more fat to make up for the new, lower, energy supply; it does not react well to high deficits from your usual energy intakes.

5.5.1 Fixed calorie reduction

A reduction of 500 to 1000kcal a day, coupled with an exercise regime, will almost certainly result in fat loss; perhaps about 0.5kg a week. However, some sources suggest a precise daily deficit of 643kcal, so it might be worth looking at where these figures come from.

Since 1g of fat is equivalent to about 9kcal, then we have:

(500kcal)/(9kcal) = 56g of fat (2 s.f.)

So a reduction of 500kcal a day means a loss of $7 \times 56 = 392$g of fat; hence, a loss of about 0.392kg of fat a week. Similarly, a daily reduction of 1000kcal would result in a loss of about 0.784kg of fat a week.

Another way to calculate the daily calorific deficit is to first choose the desired weekly fat loss, then calculate the corresponding daily calorie reduction. A maximum of fat loss to aim for is about 1kg a week, anything more could easily result in muscle loss, so it is better to aim for a safer and more realistic loss of about 0.5kg a week. Since 0.5kg of fat equates to 9kcal, we have:

(9kcal × 500g) = 4500kcal

So, dividing 4500kcal by seven gives 643kcal; the daily calorie reduction necessary to lose about 0.5kg of fat a week.

In any case, the potential problem with a fixed calorie reduction method is that it may not meet the minimum requirements of the macronutrients, essential to all sports people, or it may even far exceed such requirements. The table below shows how a fixed energy deficit would affect two very different athletes, in two very different ways.

	Athlete 1	Athlete 2
Normal daily energy intake	4287	2000
Normal daily intake less 643 calories	3644	1357

From the table, no firm conclusions should be made, as there is too little information. It is not clear whether the intake for **Athlete 1** is too high or whether the intake for **Athlete 2** is too low (though this seems likely). Nonetheless, **Athlete 1** appears to be more likely to be able to meet the necessary nutrient requirements, if not exceed them, though this does depend on many factors such as intensity, duration, age and gender. **Athlete 2**, on the other hand, seems to have a dangerously low intake, whether an athlete or not. Indeed, the resulting daily intake should instantly inform **Athlete 2** to review her eating and/or training habits thoroughly.

In the short term (perhaps the first two weeks) they will both lose about the same amount of fat or weight, but soon after that, **Athlete 2** may start to lose muscle tissue, and will also begin to be affected by all the things previously discussed in such cases. If **Athlete 1** is still consuming too many calories despite the reduction, then weight maintenance or even increase may result.

5.5.2 Fixed-percentage-reduction method

Another common method is to reduce the TDEE by a fixed percentage; normally a reduction of between 15 and 20 per cent. Provided your normal intake is not too low in the first place, this method works well; it is likely to meet the minimum macronutrient requirements (often with some to spare) and it is unlikely to lead to a dangerously high reduction. Usually, the only problem is in the unnecessary calculations.

Let's assume that a 70kg, male athlete has a TDEE of about 3000kcal a day, including exercise, and requires a minimum of 5g of carbohydrates per kg of body mass for his sport. Since he is on a fat-loss programme, he opts for the minimum fat intake of 14 per cent, and increases his protein intake to about 1.6g per kg of body mass. This athlete chooses to reduce his TDEE by 20 per cent.

Fixed-percentage-reduction method

1. Find your TDEE.
2. Calculate your minimum carbohydrate intake.
3. Calculate your amended protein intake.
4. Calculate the chosen kcal reduction percentage of the TDEE at *1.*
5. Calculate a temporary new intake by subtracting the *chosen kcal reduction percentage* (the figure at *4.*) from the TDEE (the figure at *1.*).
6. Calculate the chosen fat percentage kcal intake from the temporary new intake.
7. Find the sum of your kcal for macronutrient intakes (carbohydrate, proteins and fat) by summing the figures found at *2.*, *3.* and *6.*
8. Find your spare calories (if any) by subtracting the figure at *7.* from the figure at *5.*
9. Decide how to use the remaining calories, if applicable.
10. Check to see what your actual percentage intakes are of each macronutrient (before adding any spare calories) and pay particular attention to the fat intake; it may afford/demand more room for further reductions or allow for a higher intensity of training. The percentages can be obtained as follows:
    carbohydrates: $[(2.)/(7.)] \times 100$
    protein: $[(3.)/(7.)] \times 100$
    fat: $[(6.)/(7.)] \times 100$

Example 5.1 Minimum-requirements fat-loss method

1. TDEE is 3000kcal.
2. Carbohydrate intake is $5 \times 70 = 350$ g; hence, $4 \times 350 = 1400$kcal.
3. Protein intake $1.6 \times 70 = 112$ g; hence, $4 \times 112 = 448$kcal.
4. The chosen kcal reduction of 20 per cent is:
   $3000 \times 0.20 = 600$kcal.
5. The temporary new intake is the TDEE less the chosen kcal reduction: $3000 - 600 = 2400$kcal.
6. The chosen fat percentage intake is 14 per cent of the temporary new intake:
   $2400 \times 0.14 = 336$.
7. Total macronutrient intake so far is: $1400 + 448 + 336 = 2184$kcal.
8. Spare calories: $2400 - 2148 = 216$kcal.
9. This athlete has decided to use the spare calories as carbohydrates.
10. Carbohydrate intake: $[(1400/2184)] \times 100 \approx 64.1$ per cent.
    Protein intake: $[(448/2184)] \times 100 \approx 20.5$ per cent
    Fat intake turned out to be: $[(336/2184)] \times 100 \approx 15.4$ per cent

As you can see, with the demands of minimum carbohydrate requirements, minimum fat percentages and a recommended amount of protein, there is little flexibility; working with percentages is shown, once again, to be less reliable and unnecessarily complicated. Indeed, the calculation for the chosen fat percentage intake comes from an intake figure (the temporary new intake) that may not even be the final intake. Moreover, if the spare calories are not used, then the actual percentage deficit of the TDEE would be quite different, in the example above it would mean a reduction of over 27 per cent. See the corresponding Excel program.

This athlete did meet all minimum requirements, and even had some energy to spare. However, if some of the intakes were slightly higher, he could easily have fallen short, and the entire calculation would have needed to be adjusted and repeated. For this reason, working with a fixed-percentage reduction and then hoping all else will fall into place seems rather pointless. By now it should be glaringly obvious that the most sensible method is to begin with the minimum intakes and then work with what is left; this is what we shall look at next.

5.5.3 Minimum-requirements-considered method

This method is simpler than the previous method, and guarantees that all the minimum intakes are met.

Minimum-requirements fat-loss method

1. Find your TDEE.
2. Calculate your minimum carbohydrate intake.
3. Calculate your amended protein intake.
4. Calculate your fat intake as 14 per cent of your TDEE at *1*. This may seem strange as it will give a figure based on an intake no longer consumed. However, it makes the calculation much easier, and since this is working with the lower end of the minimum fat intake range it is unlikely to result in an excessive fat consumption.
5. Subtract the sum of *2.*, *3.* and *4.*, above, from your TDEE at *1*.
6. Subtract the figure at *5.* from the TDEE at *1*. It is advisable to subtract a minimum of about 600-700kcal to ensure an average of 0.5kg of fat loss a week.
7. Decide how to use the remaining calories, if applicable.
8. Check to see what your actual percentage intakes are of each macronutrient and pay particular attention to the fat intake; it may afford/demand more room for further deductions or allow for a higher intensity of training. The percentages can be obtained as follows.

    carbohydrates: $[(2.)/(6.)] \times 100$

    protein: $[(3.)/(6.)] \times 100$

    fat: $[(4.)/(6.)] \times 100$

Example 5.2 Minimum-requirements fat-loss method

This example is based on the athlete considered in *5.5.2*, above.

1. TDEE is 3000kcal.
2. Minimum carbohydrate intake is 1400kcal.
3. Minimum protein intake is 448kcal.
4. 14 per cent of 3000 (TDEE at *1.*) is 420.
5. 3000 - (1,400 + 448 + 420) = 732.

6. The figure obtained at *5.* is close enough to the advisable deficit of 600-700kcal, so it would be fine to deduct the entire 732kcal from *1.*, thus giving a new intake of: 3000 - 732 = 2268kcal.

7. In this case there are no remaining calories to consider.

8. Carbohydrate intake: [(1400/2268)] ×100 ≈ 61.7 per cent.

    Protein intake: [(448/2268)] × 100 ≈ 19.8 per cent

    Fat intake turned out to be: [420/2268] × 100 ≈ 18.5 per cent. This is within the required range, but also allows for an adjusted (lower) fat intake at *4.* if required.

All these percentages correspond well to the recommended intakes of the macronutrients, so this athlete is assured of getting enough good nutrition (assuming wholesome food is consumed), plenty of training fuel, and losing excess fat safely and steadily. However, there is yet one more method that is simpler still, **it is the recommended method in this text and is explained next.**

5.5.4 Fat-intake-according-BM method

Although there seems to be no generally recommended fat intake in terms of grammes per kilogramme of body mass (as there is for carbohydrates and protein), there is such a recommendation for fat loss:

*   0.5g - 1.0g of fat per kg of BM

This allows for far simpler calculations of fat intakes - indeed, the fat intake calculation is the only difference between the previous method and the one that follows.

Fat intake according to BM method

1. Find your TDEE

2. Calculate your minimum carbohydrate intake

3. Calculate your amended protein intake

4. Calculate your fat intake in the range 0.5-1.0g per kg of body mass.

5. Subtract the sum of *2.* to *4.* from your TDEE at *1.*. Note that *4.* now has two sums, the minimum and maximum values of the fat intake range.

6. Subtract the figure at **5.** from the TDEE at **1.** It is advisable to subtract a minimum of about 600-700kcal to ensure an average of 0.5kg of fat loss a week.

7. Decide how to use the remaining calories, if applicable.

8. Check to see what your actual percentage intakes are of each macronutrient and pay particular attention to the fat intake; it may afford/demand more room for further deductions or allow for a higher intensity of training. The percentages can be obtained as follows.

   carbohydrates: $[(\textbf{2.})/(\textbf{6.})] \times 100$

   protein: $[(\textbf{3.})/(\textbf{6.})] \times 100$

   fat: $[(\textbf{4.})/(\textbf{6.})] \times 100$

Example 5.3 Fat-intake-according-to-BM method

This example is based on the athlete considered in **5.5.2**, above.

1. TDEE is 3000kcal

2. Minimum carbohydrate intake is 1400kcal

3. Minimum protein intake is 448kcal

4. Fat intake range is 35-70g, which converts to 315-630kcal

5. 3000 - (1400 + 448 + 315) = 837 or

   3000 - (1400 + 448 + 630) = 522

   Covering the low and high ends of the fat intake range, respectively.

6. The figures obtained at **5.** are close enough to the advisable deficit of 600-700kcal, so it would be fine to deduct anything within the obtained range of 522-837kcal from **1.**; let's consider both the higher and lower values to see how this affects the percentage intakes: thus the new intake is in the range of 2163 and 2478kcal.

7. In this case there are no remaining calories to consider.

8. Carbohydrate intake:

   $[(1400/2478)] \times 100 \approx 56.5$ per cent, or:

   $[(1400/2163)] \times 100 \approx 64.7$ per cent

   Protein intake:

   $[(448/2478)] \times 100 \approx 18.0$ per cent, or:

   $[(448/2163)] \times 100 \approx 20.7$ per cent

Fat intake turned out to be:

[630/2478] × 100 ≈ 25.4 per cent, or:

[315/2163] × 100 ≈ 14.5 per cent, or:

Both of these figures are within the required general range of 15 to 30 per cent.

In practice, it is of course easier (and advisable) to choose just one figure from the obtained range at item 4 above.

Once again, all the intakes correspond well to the needs of the athlete, with the benefit of a simpler method. In any case, a loss of 0.5kg of fat a week is not guaranteed; it will fluctuate, and some weeks there might be no loss at all. The body cannot simply continue to lose weight, else we could theoretically disappear. However, with continued training and correct energy intake, a suitable body mass and fat percentage should be reached without any of the downfalls associated with high-energy reductions.

It is not always easy to meet all the needs described above, but if anything has to give make a trade off between:

1. your carbohydrate intake (increase) and fat intake (decrease), or
2. your carbohydrate intake (decrease) and exercise intensity and type (decrease).

Since the recommended protein intake seems to be one of the better ways to help in fat-loss programmes, it is best to allow for an increase in your carbohydrates by reducing your fat intake, though fat should not be lower than 14 per cent (item 1, above). This means that the training intensity can remain the same, or even increase; this is better since it can mean even more fat burning without loss of muscle mass - perhaps even muscle gain. Alternatively, if you are already at your minimum fat intake then you may have to lower your essential energy requirements from carbohydrates by reducing your training intensity temporarily (item 2, above).

Some sources recommend slightly lowering your protein intake, but not by less than 1.5g per kg of body mass. However, this is a waste of time as such a small adjustment will make no significant difference. For instance, a 75kg athlete on the recommended

1.6g of protein per kg of body mass will intake 120g of protein a day. If this were lowered to 1.5g of protein then the adjusted intake would be about 113g of protein a day; this only buys the athlete an extra 28kcal of carbohydrates. In any case, lowering protein intake by a significant amount is difficult to do without also adversely affecting muscle mass.

If you find that you are left with a very large number of calories to play with, say more than 1000kcal, do not be tempted to deduct all of this from your TDEE to form your new daily energy intake. The question is: does this meet your required intake of macronutrients? If not, you may need to carefully review your reasons for considering weight loss in the first place. If you are already eating wholesomely but you are not exercising at all or enough, then this is an essential consideration; without exercise fat-loss diets will not work in the long run.

Keep in mind that your TDEE and each of your macronutrient intakes are entirely dependent on your body mass, so as this changes (decreases in this case) it is important to review them regularly, at least until you reach your desired body mass.

5.6 Reasons for weight loss

Sports people are often the worst offenders when it comes to unnecessary dieting for weight or fat loss. Sometimes is it the fault of the sport because many are aesthetic, or require certain weight categories, and other times it is simply the obsessive nature of the individual. For instance, ballet dancers, especially ballerinas, are often at a dangerously low weight, yet they are encouraged, or even fiercely pressured, to lose even more weight by their instructors. Boxers will go to any extreme to *make the weight* for the weigh-in; else the bout will not take place. This often leaves them mentally and physically exhausted on the day of the fight, and greatly affects their performance and possibly their health.

It has been observed many times that those losing weight for aesthetic or weight-dependent sports are more likely to develop eating disorders than those losing weight for performance purposes alone. Indeed, the prevalence of eating disorders in élite athletes has been shown to be greater than in the general population. Furthermore, since it is far more common among female athletes, a male athlete's eating disorder may often go unnoticed.

Weight loss can occur from losing fat, bone density to a small degree, water, and muscle. Ideally though, weight loss should come primarily from the right amount of fat loss. Water levels should be balanced, and bone density and muscle mass should be increased or maintained if already at a wholesome state.

If you are losing weight simply for appearance, then you are at a higher risk of attaining an eating disorder. The danger occurs when appearance becomes an obsession, especially if it over-rides the importance of health. It is often fine, and even advisable, to increase or decrease your weight, but the primary reason must always be for the good of your long-term health, and then your performance. Appearance will no doubt change for the better anyway, provided you are losing or gaining weight in the right way and for the right reasons. For example, professional boxers are often guilty of trying too hard to remain within a certain weight category, rather than move up a weight naturally. Whatever their reasons this is always a losing battle; if nature demands a new, higher weight it is better to move up and meet the new challenges ahead or to consider retiring gracefully. Continually struggling to remain within a certain weight category often leads to eating disorders and other health problems that will inevitably affect your success. The main types of weight loss and weight gain are highlighted below:

- **negative weight gain**: weight increase mainly in the form of excessive fat
- **positive weight gain**: weight increase mainly in the form of desired and/or required lean muscle
- **negative weight loss**: a loss of weight mainly via dehydration and a loss of lean muscle
- **positive weight loss**: a loss of weight mainly in the form of excessive fat

Eating disorders are discussed in more detail in *Chapter 10*.

5.7 Dieting and eating habits

There is obviously a physiological need for us to eat, but the chosen foods need to be nutritionally balanced in order to maintain health and to reduce the chances of illness. However, the reasons for our eating habits vary greatly. In the richer parts of the world, especially the West, people have a tendency to eat as a matter of habit; food is widely available and often at any hour of the day. Social differences across cultures also play a major role in eating habits, including what is eaten, at what time and how often. It is often the pleasures of eating, rather than the physiological need to do so, that controls our consumption. Eating for pleasure is not a nutritional crime, but it is paramount for you to:

- be in control of your eating habits, rather than the other way round
- know what your aims are
- know why you have such aims
- know the best (known) ways to achieve them

Food guides

Two of the more common depictions of food guides are the **Food Triangle** (or Food Pyramid) and the **Food Plate**. The figures here use simple pictures and advice, but many such guides include full-colour photographs and specific advice about water intake, certain oils, exercise, red meat and so on, and there are even Food Triangles and Food Plates that cater for vegans, vegetarians, certain cultures, sports nutrition and many others.

Fig 5.2 Basic food triangle

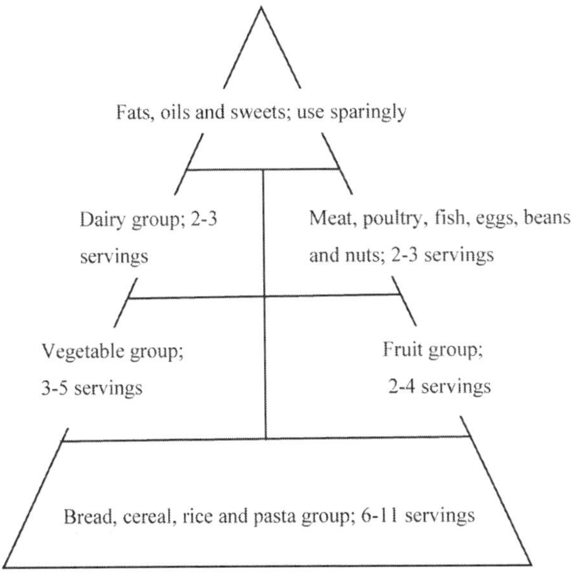

Fats, oils and sweets; use sparingly

Dairy group; 2-3 servings

Meat, poultry, fish, eggs, beans and nuts; 2-3 servings

Vegetable group; 3-5 servings

Fruit group; 2-4 servings

Bread, cereal, rice and pasta group; 6-11 servings

The first food triangle was published in Sweden in 1974, but the most commonly used one became the one proposed in 1992 by the US Department of Agriculture (USDA) - Figure 5.2 is effectively the same as this. It was not updated until 2005, and then replaced by a food plate (called MyPlate) in 2011. The idea is to make it simple for individuals to choose a balanced and wholesome diet, with or without any great knowledge of nutrition, and in this regard the older triangle is perhaps an easier choice over certain food plates. The Food Triangles normally include a range of serving suggestions for each food group, though these vary according to the type and/or the country for which it is intended. Some Food Plates, on the other hand, are based on percentages, and this is where they may fall short; refer to the example below to see how some types of Food Plate are used to assess an individual's apparent nutritional shortcomings and overindulgences.

Fig. 5.3 Basic food plate

Example 5.7 Food Plate

The number of servings for each food group is recorded and then converted into a percentage of the total number of servings; these percentages are then compared against the recommended percentage intakes. The following tabulated data is a real example of a man's intake for one day.

Food group	Servings	Recommended percentage	Actual percentage of that group
Bread/cereals group	7	33	35 - too high
Fruit and vegetables	5	33	25 - too low
Meat and fish	4	12	20 - too high
Dairy products	3	15	15 - just right
Fats and sugars	1	7	05 - too low
Total	20		

The percentages in the last column are used to determine which food groups need to be increased or decreased, or which (if any) are just right, by comparing them to the corresponding recommended percentages in the third column. The actual percentage of each group (fourth column entries) was attained by dividing the number of servings of each food group by the total number of servings and then multiplying the result by 100. For instance, there were seven servings of the bread/cereal group and the total number of servings was 20, so:

$$(7/20) \times 100 = 35$$

Hence, 35 per cent of the diet was from the bread/cereal group.

Food guide analysis

Now, according to the guide the individual from *Example 5.7* needs to consume:

a) a little less bread and cereals

b) far more fruit and vegetables

c) far less meat and fish

d) more fats and sugars

Comparing these findings with the recommended intakes of the food triangle shows conflicting results; for example, items *a)* and *b)* are within the recommended ranges according to many Food Triangles, yet according to the Food Plate, they need to be reviewed. So let us consider what happens when the intakes are changed to the following:

Food group	Servings	Recommended percentage	Actual percentage of that group
Bread/cereals group	6	33	28.6 - too low
Fruit and vegetables	8	33	38.1 - too high
Meat and fish	2	12	9.5 - too low
Dairy products	3	15	14.3 - too low
Fats and sugars	2	7	9.5 - too high
Total	21		

The bread and cereals group has been decreased from seven servings to six, the fruit and vegetable group has been increased from five servings to eight, the meat and fish group has been decreased from four servings to two, and the fats and sugar group has been increased from one serving to two. Referring to the two tables the following significant observations can be made:

- The bread and cereal group is now considered too low, even though it has been altered by only one serving and previously it was too high.
- The fruit and vegetables group has changed from too low to too high; though this has been increased by three servings.
- The meat and fish group has changed from too high to too low.
- The dairy products group has changed from 'just right' to too low, even though the number of servings has not been altered; however, in fairness, 14.3 per cent is close enough to the targeted 15 per cent.
- The fats and sugars group has changed from too low to too high, even though it has been increased by only one serving.
- The total number of servings has increased from 20 to 21, which in most cases should not be significant, at least in terms of the difference.

The problem with this method is that each serving is a percentage of the total number of servings, so any change to the number of servings for a food group will affect *all* food groups. For instance, on reviewing the observations above, you might be tempted to simply reduce the fruit and vegetables group by one serving, but doing so will not even correct this group, let alone the others. Further tweaking may eventually bring all servings within acceptable bounds, but consider the number of extra calculations that might be necessary to get there. It is also worth noting that a very low number of total servings may still read as acceptable, even though it may well be nutritionally wanting. The same applies to very high numbers of total servings; just try doubling the number of servings for each food group in either of the tables above and see what happens to the results… absolutely nothing.

Ironically, someone with the knowledge of how to calculate such intake percentages may have a harder time attaining the recommended balance than someone who simply chooses according to the visual proportions without a second thought. Indeed, most food plates are now merely visual guides rather than strict percentages, but even this is misleading and difficult to follow. There seems to be no simple way to read food plates. If, for instance, a particular food plate is a guide for a day's consumption then how is segmenting each food group easier than numerical guides on portions of each? It will mean reverting to percentages, which is cumbersome, or simply considering the recommended number of portions. In either case, it seems that *plates* (or triangles) are unnecessary.

In short, food guides are precisely that: *guides*, and should therefore be taken as such. In any case, any serious sportsperson should be practising an individualistic approach, and if you have read this far then you are already way ahead of such guides any way.; hence why no sports nutrition food triangle was used as Figure 5.2.

Diet and metabolism

If the body is restricted to a very low calorie intake (or perhaps no calories at all) for several hours it reacts by entering a state referred to as **fasting mode**, also commonly, but inappropriately, called starvation mode (see *famine response* below). The time this takes to occur varies from person to person, and it also depends on the level of energy restriction; however, it seems that **most would certainly enter fasting mode after five hours of no intake of energy** at all.

The body will initially obtain energy from the contents of the digestive tract and the glycogen reserves stored in muscle and liver cells. However, if the energy restriction is too much for too long it will eventually resort to taking its energy from the proteins within muscle tissue - thus adversely affecting lean muscle mass.

Energy-restricted diets will eventually lower the metabolism because the body needs a way to become more efficient while it has been forced to function on less fuel; this is perhaps especially true of very low-energy diets of 800 to 1000kcal a day, and perhaps even diets of TDEE less a significant percentage - say, 25 per cent. This in turn will eventually reduce the initial weight loss of about half to 1kg a week in the earlier part of dieting, to less than 1kg a month. The time taken for metabolic adaptation to occur during dieting depends on the individual, but it would normally happen in a matter of a few weeks rather than months. Furthermore, it seems to be more pronounced the greater the calorie reduction, but whether this relationship is linear is still not certain. Nevertheless, if moderate energy restriction is coupled with an exercise programme, particularly one that includes resistance exercise, there appears to be little or no metabolic adaptation during dieting, which is in agreement with the method recommended at **5.5.4**, above. Another benefit of combining a moderate energy-restricted diet with exercise is that it produces the same or better fat-loss results than energy reduction alone, with the added benefit of an improved physique and level of fitness. In any case, high energy restrictions will adversely affect your vitamin and mineral intake as well as your training capacity and even your will to do so.

When the desired weight has been achieved and energy levels have been returned to normal, the metabolism will also soon return to normal. However, your *normal* metabolism may have changed. It may be lower if you have lost a considerable amount of body mass, or it may be higher if your level of fitness has greatly improved in the process of losing weight (refer also to 5.1). That said, many do not actually need to go on fat-loss diets; they simply need to *change* their diet and eating habits. We often confuse thirst signals for hunger signals, so try some fluids (even just water) before reaching straight for solids. It is advisable to have a substantial and wholesome breakfast every day; numerous studies have shown that those who regularly eat breakfast in the morning consistently weigh less than those who eat it less often or not at all. If you feel hungry within a couple of hours of a full meal, then it may be that that your meal simply did not provide enough energy and/or the GL was too high.

Crash diets are any diets that are severely low in energy; many are even lower than 800kcal a day, and literally border on starvation. Despite their quick results in the early stages of the diet, they are dangerous and do not work in the long term. Training will be difficult or impossible because of a lack of energy, and may be hazardous because training on such low energy may cause faintness. Furthermore, they are nutritionally inadequate, to put it mildly, and most of the weight loss will not be in the form of fat anyway. Crash diets are never a good idea, even for a few days, so despite the many Internet sites and other sources that advocate them, avoid crash diets or any other lose-weight-fast methods at all costs.

Famine response

If glucose is not available from the diet, it can be obtained from the breakdown of glycogen that is stored in small quantities in the liver and muscles; this reserve can provide glucose for about six hours. When this reserve is exhausted, glucose can be obtained from the breakdown of fats and eventually from protein; **starvation is the state when protein is the only fuel source available to the body**. This eventually leads to muscle wastage and the malfunction of vital organs, and ultimately leads to death.

Rapid weight loss owing to dehydration.

Dehydration causes a reduced cardiac output (see *Appendix B*), reduced plasma volume and slower waste removal, all of which affect health and performance. As will be mentioned in the next chapter, *Fluid Essentials*, weight lost via dehydration is very short-term, and has numerous adverse effects on health - a prime example of negative weight loss.

Calorie counting

The current trend seems to be anti-calorie-counting. This seems strange, since any weight/fat loss diet simply will not work unless more calories are burnt than are consumed. It is true that calorie counting can be off-putting and it is very tedious at first, but unfortunately there is little option. Numerous studies have shown that people grossly understate or exaggerate their calorie intake, so unless you know your intake it will be very difficult to know where your problem lies should your diet fail.

Losing fat takes discipline, there is no other option. You need discipline in your diet, in your attitude and in your exercise regime. As time goes on, though, the calorie counting will become easier and eventually unnecessary - unless of course the unwanted fat returns.

5.8 Fat cells and fat loss

The number of fat cells in the human body is normally predetermined by genetics; the quantity we are born with increases until we reach puberty, then fat-cell production stops, although about 10 per cent are renewed annually, regardless of age and BMI. According to estimates, the number of fat cells settles at about 26,000,000,000 (26 billion) for men and about 35,000,000,000 (35 billion) for women, with upper limits for both men and women of between 40 billion and 60 billion. However, if obesity occurs during childhood or adolescence, the settled number of fat cells in adulthood can be considerably higher - three to five times more than average. Moreover, the number of fat cells may also increase (**fat cell hyperplasia**) during adulthood if the diet is consistently poor for long enough to exhaust the capacity of the existing fat cells; some experts say that this occurs when the BMI is greater than 40 *(see also **4.2, Body Mass Index (BMI)** for the limitations of the BMI)*. For instance, a person who is just 1.62 meters tall with a body mass of 105kg has a BMI of just over 40.

In a very recent study, the number of fat cells increased by an average of about 2.5 billion in just eight weeks of overeating, and the fat mass increased by about 2kg in the upper body and about 1.5kg in the lower. Nevertheless, it should be noted that many papers, including several fairly recent ones, disagree with the idea of fat cell production post-adolescence. Such papers propose that fat cells can only increase in mass and volume (**fat cell hypertrophy**), and some further suggest that existing cells (that previously did not hold fat) may be used to offset an ever-increasing fat storage demand.

Fat cells vary in volume and mass depending on their location in the body, and each weighs an average 0.6 micrograms (mcg), but can range from about 0.2mcg to about 0.9mcg. We cannot reduce the number of fat cells we have without liposuction, but we can shrink them - in other words, reduce their mass. The following theoretical example demonstrates how the number of fat cells alone gives little idea of what they really mean without more information on the person concerned. The results are all that really matter here; the prerequisite mathematics and other calculations can be ignored, but have been included for the sake of completion.

 Prerequisite for fat cell examples

Consider the size of the numbers that we are discussing:

1 thousand million (1 billion) = 1,000,000,000 = 10^9

Consider also, the mass that we are discussing:

$1mcg = 0.000001g$ (or $10^{-6}g$)

So the average mass of a fat cell in grammes is:

$0.6mcg = 0.6/10^6 g$

The lower and higher masses are:

$0.2mcg = 0.2/10^6 g$

$0.9mcg = 0.9/10^6 g$

 Example 5.8.1 Fat cell number and mass only

In this example we are comparing two different possibilities of the *same* individual who has:

a) the average, 26 billion cells, with an average cell mass of 0.6mcg

b) an above average, 50 billion fat cells, with an average mass of 0.2mcg

In case *a)* the total fat mass accounts for $(0.6/10^6) \times (26 \times 10^9) = 15,600g$, or 15.6kg. Yet even though the number of fat cells in case *b)* is nearly twice that of case *a)*, fat only accounts for $(0.2/10^6) \times (50 \times 10^9) = 10,000g$, or 10kg. Needless to say, the mass and number of fat cells mean little without more information about an individual's age, gender and body mass at the very least *(see the next example)*.

 Example 5.8.2 Fat cell number, mass and other information

In this example we are comparing three different possibilities of the same 46-year-old man who has a body mass of 76kg and who has:

a) The average, 26 billion cells, with an average cell mass of 0.9mcg. So fat accounts for about 23.4kg of total body mass, which is about (23.4/76) = 0.31, or 31 per cent.

b)   An above average, 40 billion fat cells, with an average mass of 0.6mcg. So fat accounts for about 24kg of total body mass, or about 32 per cent.

c)   An above average, 60 billion fat cells, with an average mass of 0.2mcg. So fat accounts for about 12kg of total body mass, or about 16 per cent.

In cases *a)* and *b)* his body fat, at 31 per cent and 32 per cent, respectively, is way too high for a man (regardless of age), even though in case *a)* the number of fat cells is average. In case *c)*, despite having a massive 60 billion fat cells, his total body fat is at a healthy 16 per cent.

If nothing else, we hope that these examples offer some encouragement to those who struggle to lose weight, or who have given up altogether. We have shown that even a person with more than double the average number of fat cells can still greatly improve his body composition. Furthermore, we have also shown that although genetics usually predetermines our number of fat cells attained by adolescence, its accountability for excessive body mass problems is very limited. Many people who are overweight erroneously think that their body mass is *natural* and therefore attempting weight loss is pointless; this is not true...it is always worth the effort.

6 Fluid Essentials

Advice on fluid intake is often misleading, vague, conflicting or a combination of these. The intakes of macronutrients, covered in **Chapters 2** to **4** inclusive, are very important regarding training results and performance, but poor intakes of these are rarely life-threatening. However, correct fluid intakes are vital, especially for endurance sports. Loosely speaking, the two main concerns of fluid intake are:

- **hyponatraemia:** low blood salt level owing to abnormal fluid retention from drinking too much
- **dehydration:** net fluid losses from drinking too little

In other words, drinking too much or drinking too little, since either of these can be a serious risk to health. Nevertheless, as we shall see, these definitions address only part of the issue; the frequency and type of fluid ingested is equally important.

The general aim is to maintain **fluid balance** as best we can; fluid balance refers to the amount of fluid loss being equal to the amount of fluid intake. This *amount* of fluid varies significantly from person to person, depending on several factors such as fitness level, exercise intensity and duration, ambient temperature and humidity. The body works continuously to meet the fluid balance, since fluid is lost and gained through normal physiological actions throughout the entire day. Apart from drinking, fluid intake also comes from food (0.5-1L a day), and rather less obviously, from the metabolism of food (0.25-0.4L a day). Fluid loss, on the other hand, occurs mainly through urination, but much less noticeably through respiration, perspiration and other physiological means:

- urination: about 1500ml/day in adults
- perspiration: 400-800ml/day in adults, though this is highly contentious as measuring perspiration loss is not easy - which is why it is often referred to as *insensible fluid losses.*
- lungs: 400ml/day
- faeces: about 100ml/day in adults.
- vaginal secretions: about 50ml/day.

At first glance, meeting the fluid balance seems simple; just sum the outputs above and use the result as the fluid intake. Unfortunately, attaining fluid intake, especially for sports people, is not so simple.

This chapter begins with a brief discussion on electrolytes followed by a short but detailed look at human body temperature, including measuring devices and points of measurement and the difference between hyperthermia and hypothermia and first aid on how to treat them. There is a concise explanation on how to measure fluid deficit and then a detailed explanation on the different types of sport fluid and how to make them. The fluid cycle (before, during and after exercise) is also fully explained before the chapter closes with some useful information on alcohol, especially regarding dehydration and how *units of alcohol* can be a very deceptive measure.

6.1 Electrolytes

Electrolytes are very small mineral salts that help a variety of functions in the body, including major contributions to muscle contraction, fluid transportation, nerve impulses and ATP. There are many electrolytes, including sodium, chlorine, potassium, calcium and magnesium. When you exercise you lose electrolytes in your perspiration - particularly sodium and potassium - and the more you perspire, the more you lose. These lost electrolytes must be replaced to keep the concentrations of your body fluids constant.

The body continually aims to keep a balance between its water and electrolyte levels. For example, when we perspire to an extent that sodium levels become too low, the kidneys produce more urine, which restores the balance because the amount of water in the blood has been lowered. Similarly, when sodium levels become too high, the kidneys produce less urine and we receive thirst signals and respond by drinking; thus restoring the balance once again.

Sodium chloride (salt)

In terms of chemistry, **salt** is the crystallised form of a combination of strictly two elements, sodium and chlorine; hence, **sodium is *not* a formal term for salt**. Common salt, or **table salt** is about 99.9 per cent sodium chloride, plus very small amounts of other minerals, but this distinction is unnecessary for our purposes, so from here on salt will always refer to table salt.

When salt is ingested, these elements become separated, and when the levels of sodium become too high the body retains too much water so the volume of body fluid increases, consequently effecting an increase in blood pressure (**hypertension**). In the UK, the **guideline daily amounts** (GDA) for salt is no more than 7g for men and 5g for women, but the mass of chlorine is about one and a half times that of sodium - in other words, salt is in a 1:1.5 ratio of sodium to chlorine. Therefore, dividing these GDAs by 2.5 (the sum of 1 and 1.5) gives the approximate equivalent of the GDA for sodium intake:

> **men: daily sodium intake should not exceed 2.8g**
>
> **women: daily sodium intake should not exceed 2g**

It is important to know this since many packaged foods conceal their amount of salt by giving only the sodium content on the nutritional information label, and since many people think that sodium is just a formal name for salt, it makes it seem that the salt content is much lower than it actually is. The following sub-section explains this and related issues in more detail. See also *7.2 Food labelling*.

6.1.1 Calculating sodium in food

Some food packages give the amount of salt and sodium separately (or even just the sodium), in which case there may be no need for any calculations. However, some packages hide the true amount of sodium by giving only the amount per 100g and not by a typical portion size. To add to the complication, some food packages give only the salt content, so finding the amount of sodium is even more complicated.

Calculating sodium or salt according to portion sizes

The calculations below are based on the assumption that the nutritional content of a particular food is given per 100g. This section is concerned only with the salt and sodium content, but the method can of course be used for any nutritional facts provided. Since we are working in grammes, the salt or sodium content must also be in grammes before you make any calculations. Sodium is often given in milligrammes (mg), in which case you will first need to divide the number by 1000 to convert it into grammes, e.g. 180mg is 0.18g;

1. divide the salt or sodium content (given per 100g) by 100.
2. multiply the *1.* by the portion size

Example

A food item package might tells us that there is 0.5g of sodium per 100g, but the portion is 180g. Therefore:

1. 0.5/100 = 0.005
2. 180 × 0.005 = 0.9

So in this case the sodium content is 0.9g per portion.

Calculating the amount of sodium when only salt is given

These days it is uncommon for the amount of salt to be provided on a food package without also giving the amount of sodium. No matter, the calculation is simple:

- divide the amount of salt by 2.5 to give the amount of sodium

Similarly, the calculation for salt given only the amount of sodium is equally simple:

- multiply the amount of sodium by 2.5 to give the amount of salt

However, some find it confusing if they have to work out the amount of sodium if given only the salt content per 100 grammes, especially if the portion size is more or less than 100g. In fact it is just a combination of the ideas just discussed above:

1. divide the salt or sodium content (given per 100g) by 100.
2. multiply the figure found at *1.* by the portion size.
3. divide the figure found at *2.* by 2.5.

Example

Consider a particular brand of flavoured oats that contains 1.28g of salt per 100g, but the portion size is only 35g.

1. $1.28/100 = 0.0128$
2. $0.0128 \times 35 = 0.448$
3. $0.448/2.5 = 0.1792$

So the amount of sodium per 35g portion is about 0.18g, and out of interest, the salt content is therefore 0.45g (from 0.18×2.5) per portion.

To add to the problem, nutritional information labels on packaged foods often give a misleading suggested serving size; they are noticeably small, especially for sportspeople.

Example

A particular brand of 'ready to eat' vegetable curry contains 0.57g of sodium per 100g serving. However, a sportsperson could easily consume the whole 300g-packet, which means the sodium content (of only this part of the meal) is already three times the serving suggestion (0.57×3), i.e. 1.71g of sodium or about 4.3g of salt. This is over half the daily GDA of sodium for men and nearly all the daily GDA of sodium for women.

Potassium, on the other hand, seems to have the opposite effect on blood pressure to sodium. It has been shown that high potassium levels lower blood pressure, perhaps because it helps the body to cope with excess sodium. However, the best results seem to come from lowering salt intake and increasing intakes of potassium, **calcium** and **magnesium**; these are all widely distributed in (among other foods) milk or a combination of cereals, vegetables (especially greens) and fruit. See also *Chapter 7*.

6.2 Human body temperature

The so-called normal body temperatures that we are familiar with are generally given for healthy, non-dieting or non-fasting adults, who are dressed comfortably and in a room that is at room temperature (22.7°C to 24.4°C). Moreover, the measurement is taken during the morning, but not soon after rising. Yet normal human body temperature depends on several things, especially the:

- point on/in the body at which the measurement is made
- time of day
- level of activity of the person
- individual

There is no single temperature that represents a normal or healthy temperature for all people under all circumstances, regardless of the point of measurement. In samples of normal adult men and women, the temperature, depending on the point of measurement, ranges significantly:

- oral: 33.2°C to 38.2°C
- rectal: 34.4°C to 37.8°C
- axillary (armpit): 35.5°C 37.0°C

Moreover, nobody has one precise temperature at every moment of the day, temperatures rise and lower throughout the day. For instance, **normal human body temperature** (taken orally) is about **36.8°C ±0.7°C**. Hence, any oral temperature between **36.1°C** and **37.5°C** is likely to be normal. The commonly accepted average *core body temperature* (taken internally) is 37.0°C; **core temperature** is the operating temperature of an organism, specifically in deep structures of the body such as the liver.

Temperature changes

Body temperature changes for several reasons, such as when people are hungry, tired or cold; it is lowest about two hours before waking which is why we often feel cold when we wake, even on fairly warm days. Temperature also changes according to activities and external factors, and it even varies with the seasons.

An individual's body temperature typically changes by about 0.5°C from one day to the next, and even between its highest and lowest points on the same day. So certain temperatures might be normal at one point in the day but not at another. For example, it might be normal to have a temperature of 37.4°C (taken orally) in the middle of the day, yet this may be considered too high in the morning for most individuals.

Body temperature is also sensitive to hormones, which why a woman's temperature varies with the menstrual cycle. During ovulation a woman's *basal body temperature* rises by up to 0.5°C; **basal body temperature** is the lowest temperature, usually during sleep, of a living person.

An increase in fitness levels also increases the amount of daily variation in body temperature. However, a noticeable increase in body temperature usually requires strenuous exercise and/or exercise sustained over a considerable time. Our body temperature will also increase after eating or drinking, but will decrease in those on calorie-restricted diets, especially if the calorie intake is very low. Alcohol reduces the amount of daily change, and slightly lowers daytime temperatures, but causes a noticeable rise in night-time temperatures. As we age, our average body temperature and the amount of daily variability tends to decrease.

Point of measurement and measuring devices

The traditional **glass thermometers** contain mercury or other substances that are poisonous so they are not recommended, particularly soon after training. **Forehead thermometer strips** are wanting in accuracy, and give only an approximate local reading anyway; moreover, readings are easily affected by the ambient air temperature and local circulation of the subject. **Otic (ear) thermometers** are quick and easy to use and can return a reading within a few seconds, which makes them popular for use with children. However, since there are some concerns for the accuracy of otic thermometers designed for home use, it is perhaps best to use them only for observing trends in body temperature; they are not recommended for identifying fevers. The home-use **electronic thermometers**, which are made from plastic and use a metal sensor, are generally a much safer choice. They are also more accurate since they can be placed in the armpit which is much less affected by ambient temperatures.

Oral temperatures are influenced by drinking, chewing, smoking and breathing with the mouth open. Consuming cold food and drinks will reduce oral temperatures, whereas smoking, chewing gum or consuming warm or hot foods and drinks will raise oral temperatures. For these reasons, **the subject must not have consumed anything**, chewed gum or smoked for at least **15 or 20 minutes before an oral temperature is taken**. **Rectal temperature** examination is the traditional gold standard measurement used to estimate the core body temperature; it is normally about 0.5°C higher than an oral temperature taken from the same person at the same time. **Skin-based** temperature varies more than others, and is also more influenced by outside factors, such as clothing and air temperature, so devices that measure skin-based temperatures are best avoided.

Hyperthermia and treatment

A body temperature **at or above about 40°C is a life-threatening** medical emergency that requires immediate treatment. Common symptoms include headache, confusion and fatigue. If the subject is dehydrated yet perspiring, then dry, red skin may also be a symptom. In a medical setting, mild hyperthermia is commonly called **heat exhaustion** or heat prostration; severe hyperthermia is called **heat stroke**. **Treatment** involves cooling and rehydrating the body. This may be done through:

- moving the subject away from direct sunlight to a cooler area
- drinking water
- removing clothing that might keep heat close to the body
- sitting the subject in front of a fan
- bathing in tepid or cool water, or even just washing the face and other exposed areas of skin

Hypothermia and treatment

In hypothermia, body temperature drops below that required for normal metabolism and bodily functions. In humans, this is usually caused by excessive exposure to cold air or water. Symptoms usually appear when the body's core temperature drops by 1-2°C below an individual's normal temperature, but is often **defined as occurring when the body temperature drops below 35°C**; mild hypothermia may start at higher body temperatures. Severe hypothermia requires urgent medical treatment. Shivering is perhaps the best and most obvious guide to telling the severity of the condition. If the person is able to stop shivering on his own, then hypothermia is likely to be mild, but if he cannot, it is at least moderate and may even be severe. **Hypothermia is treated by** gently warming the subject in the order that follows:

1. Move the subject to somewhere warm as soon as possible, preferably indoors.
2. Remove any wet clothing from the subject and dry them.
3. Wrap them in blankets or anything to hand (towels, coats, etc.) - the head and torso are priorities.
4. The body heat of another can really help. Have them sit between two people if possible or hold them if necessary.

If they are able, once warmed a little, have them gently increase activity; *not* to the point of perspiration mind, as this will cool them down again. Warm drinks (not alcoholic) or high energy foods, such as chocolate, will also help warm them.

The **wrong treatment of hypothermia** can be very dangerous or even fatal:

- **Do not warm** a subject (especially an elderly one) **using a bath**, as it can cause a stroke or heart attack.
- **Do not apply direct heat** (hot water, heating pad, etc.) **to the limbs**; it forces cold blood back to the major organs and will worsen the condition.
- Contrary to common belief, **do not give the subject alcohol**, as this actually decreases the body's ability to retain heat.
- **Do not rub or massage the subject's skin**. This may cause the blood vessels to widen which in turn decreases the body's ability to retain heat; in extreme cases it can cause a heart attack.

6.3 Dehydration

When we exercise, we can use up a lot of water from our bodies, especially through perspiration, but significant amounts can also be lost through respiration. The body's main method of cooling, and hence maintaining the safe temperature range, is via perspiration. Water is carried to your skin via your blood capillaries, and as it evaporates you lose heat - the heat you generated from exercising in the first place. Most of the heat energy we are referring to is via conduction, i.e. heat energy transferred from one region or material to another. Some heat is also lost via convection (heat transfer through fluids and gases) and radiation (every substance continually emits and gains heat energy via radiation), but very little in comparison. Exercising, especially vigorously, is one way to use body fluid at an accelerated rate; it must be replaced in good time and with the correct type and amount.

A person is considered dehydrated when there is a one per cent or greater reduction in body mass caused by fluid loss. The initial sign of dehydration is thirst, though this by itself is not a cause for concern.

6.3.1 Symptoms and effect of dehydration

Mild dehydration occurs at a one-to-three per cent decrease in body mass caused by fluid loss. Symptoms include:

- dizziness
- headaches
- dry mouth, lips and eyes
- dark yellow urine

Passing urine in small amounts, and fewer than three or four times a day, may also indicate mild-to-moderate dehydration. This may be caused by too little fluid intake throughout the day, or it may be because you are not replenishing correctly during or after exercising. Keep in mind also that dehydration is cumulative; you can become dehydrated over a period of successive days if you fail to rehydrate between training. This emphasises the importance of post-exercise hydration, and general fluid intake.

Urine that is light yellow in colour indicates that you are within one per cent of the optimum hydration levels; however, if you are taking vitamin B_2 supplements or supplements that include it, your urine will appear a bright fluorescent yellow.

Moderate dehydration occurs at a three-to-five per cent decrease in body mass caused by fluid loss; the symptoms are often the same as those of mild dehydration, but to a greater degree. Constipation is common, but this is perhaps the least of the potential problems; kidney function may be affected, and damage to the liver, joints and muscles may also occur. When too much fluid is lost, blood volume decreases, yet blood needs to flow to the muscles whilst exercising and to the surface of the skin to carry heat away. As a consequence, the more dehydrated you become the less you are able to perspire and cool down, which is why moderate dehydration it is the main cause of heat exhaustion.

Severe dehydration occurs at a five per cent or greater decrease in body mass caused by fluid loss. There are many symptoms, including:

- dry skin
- an inability to urinate
- a weak pulse
- a rapid heartbeat
- cold hands and feet (even though the ambient temperature may be warm)
- seizures

A loss of more than 10 per cent in body mass owing to fluid loss is life-threatening; urgent medical attention is required. However, dehydration problems should never be allowed to become any worse than mild dehydration, at which stage any exercise in progress should cease immediately and gradual replenishment should begin; the advice is the same as that in *6.6.3 Post-training fluid*.

6.3.2 Dehydration and performance

There is clear evidence that dehydration can adversely affect performance. As usual, there are individual factors, but it appears that most consideration should be given to the conditions in which you are exercising and to the duration and intensity:

- **Training for up to 90 minutes in temperate conditions (20-21°C):** a body mass reduction of one-to-two per cent is likely, but no significantly adverse effect on performance should occur.
- **Training for over 90 minutes in temperate conditions:** a greater than two per cent reduction in body mass and a significantly adverse effect on performance; aerobic capacity will probably decrease by 10 per cent - but maybe as much as 20 per cent.
- **Training for up to 60 minutes in hot conditions (30-31°C):** a body mass reduction of one to two per cent is likely, but no significantly adverse effect on performance should occur.
- **Training for over 60 minutes in hot conditions:** a greater than two per cent reduction in body mass and a significantly adverse effect on performance; aerobic capacity will probably decrease by 10 per cent - but maybe by as much as 20 per cent.

- **Training in cold conditions (5-10⁰C):** in such conditions, the time it takes for a one-to-two per cent reduction in body mass has not been clearly established - though it will certainly take longer than 90 minutes. If training in low temperatures, especially below freezing, hypothermia may be the bigger concern.

As you would expect, the adverse effects of fluid loss will become more and more aggravated as the percentage of body mass reduction increases. By the time a body mass has been reduced by five per cent, the aerobic performance will have decreased by 30 per cent. This amount of body mass reduction is already at the door of severe dehydration, so exercising should have ceased long before this stage. Nonetheless, information on the adverse effects on performance owing to dehydration should not cause you to flood your body with fluids; this was a huge problem in the recent past (and may still be). During the 1990s such information caused many athletes to drink way too much fluid - and often the wrong type - and frequently resulted in athletes suffering from hyponatraemia. The best advice is also the most simple: **drink according to thirst**, or drink *ad libitum* (Latin: 'according to pleasure'). Your senses are more reliable and accurate, and much cheaper!

These days many electronic scales include hydration levels as well as body mass and fat percentage, but hydration levels are an estimate based on a mathematical calculation that already includes an unreliable fat percentage figure. In any case, the information is not necessary unless you are severely dehydrated, in which case this is a job for medical professionals. The more important information is to know if your before-and-after body mass, known as fluid deficit, has reduced by more than one per cent from fluid loss , i.e. *are you dehydrating?* This is covered in the next sub-section.

Fluid deficit
Fluid deficit is the amount of water loss that occurs during exercise; it is the simple calculation of pre-exercise body mass less post-exercise body mass. It is worth noting that if the deficit is negative, then your fluid intake before or during exercise (or both) was excessive. Fluid loss depends on:

- exercise intensity
- exercise duration
- ambient temperature and humidity
- individual body chemistry

Some sources suggest that during an hour's exercise an average person losses about one litre of fluid, more in hot and humid conditions. However, marathon runners could easily lose over two litres of fluid in hot and humid conditions; extreme endurance athletes will often lose much more. Furthermore, individual factors should not be underestimated. Levels of fluid loss depend on:

- body mass and body size: small-framed lighter people perspire less
- fitness levels: fitter people will perspire more readily owing to better thermoregulation
- acclimatisation: those acclimatised will also perspire more readily
- individual factor: some seem to perspire more than others
- sex: women tend to perspire less, not just because they generally have a smaller frame, but they also tend to have a better economy in fluid loss

Calculating fluid loss percentage

Pre-exercise body mass should be calculated in minimum clothing and *after* urination, whereas post-exercise body mass should be taken with minimum clothing, towel-dried and *before* urination.

1. note your pre-exercise body mass
2. note your post-exercise body mass
3. find your fluid deficit: subtract *2.* from *1.* - *not* the other way round
4. divide the answer from *3.* by your pre-training body mass *1.*
5. multiply your answer from *4.* by 100

Example

Assume an athlete has a pre-training body mass of 64kg and a post-training body mass of 63kg. Following the steps above gives:

Step 1, 2 and 3: 64kg - 63kg = 1kg

Step 4: 1kg/64kg = 0.016 (3dp)

Step 5: 0.016 × 100 = 1.6

So this athlete has a fluid deficit of 1kg, which corresponds to a body mass reduction of about 1.6 per cent; by definition this means that the athlete has mild dehydration.

It is a good idea to know your dehydration figures in advance of your training - at least the figures that represent one, two and three per cent body mass reduction.

Calculating dehydration figures

1. One per cent of your BM: multiply your body mass by 0.01, and subtract this result from your body mass.
2. Two per cent of your BM: multiply your body mass by 0.02 (as above).
3. Three per cent of your BM: multiply your body mass by 0.03 (as above).

Example

Consider the athlete in the previous example; the results are given to one decimal place and are followed by the dehydration diagnosis, in brackets.

1. One per cent of BM: 64kg × 0.01 = 0.6kg. So 64kg - 0.6kg = 63.4kg (acceptable).
2. Two per cent of BM: 64kg × 0.02 = 1.3kg. So 64kg - 1.3kg = 62.7kg (mild).
3. Three per cent of BM: 64kg × 0.03 = 1.9kg. So 64kg - 1.9kg = 62.1kg (low end of moderate).

6.3.3 Shell suits

The use of shell suits or any other type of clothing that prevents heat loss is extremely dangerous. The body needs to cool down, yet such clothing intentionally causes the body temperature to rise, causing more and more fluid loss via excessive perspiration. You will inevitably become dehydrated, and there have been numerous occasions when athletes (many from élite military forces) suffered serious consequences, including many fatalities. In any case, using such clothing will hinder your performance caused by early fatigue, and any body mass loss will be purely fluid, not fat.

This means that as soon as you next eat or drink, your body mass will immediately return to what it was before.

If you cannot make your required body mass for a competition, then it is better to wait until you can. In certain sports, such as boxing, it might be simpler (and certainly healthier) to move into a different, normally higher, weight category. As we age, our body mass naturally increases, so if you are already in good condition, the struggle to force your mass down is a tussle with nature and may be so exhausting that you will be utterly drained come the day of your performance. If the body mass loss is gradual and not overly demanding then it may be all right, but rapidly forcing your body mass to meet a target will be particularly demanding and definitely inadvisable.

6.4 Hyponatraemia

The kidneys can adjust to varying levels of water intake, but will need time to adjust to a much-increased amount of fluid. This is why endurance athletes need to increase their fluid intake gradually. Many people that are new to endurance training think guzzling copious amounts of fluid is good hydration; it is not. Whilst dark coloured urine is a sign that you are dehydrated, urine that is very clear (like water) is a sign that you may be drinking too much, and this may overtax the kidneys and lead to hyponatraemia - when the level of electrolytes, especially sodium, in the blood is too low. It is potentially fatal because the excess water may lower the amount of sodium in the body's cells, which may in turn cause the brain to swell. Hyponatraemia is generally rare, but is most likely to occur in athletes partaking in endurance training or events lasting over two hours and in hot conditions, such as marathons, triathlons and elite military training, and when participants drink plain water (electrolyte-free) in excess of their rates of perspiration. Small-framed athletes that drink large amounts of plain water are most at risk since their perspiration rates are naturally low. There is no benefit in drinking more than we perspire, during training or otherwise.

6.4.1 Symptoms and effect of hyponatraemia

In mild hyponatraemia some of the core symptoms are:

- nausea
- lethargy
- mild headaches

In mild cases, the subject should stop training immediately and consume a sport drink that includes electrolytes (one or two 330ml cans should be enough); if the symptoms persist, professional medical attention is required. It is important to note that these mild symptoms of hyponatraemia are the same as, or similar to, those of dehydration; so **be careful not to treat dehydration as hyponatraemia**. This is the reason that a sports drink is suggested, rather than salty food, because if the subject has been wrongly diagnosed the treatment would be the same anyway. Offering salty foods, as some sources suggest, when the subject really needed fluids, would only aggravate the condition.

If the subject's nausea turns to vomiting, or if it includes any of the symptoms below, the subject requires immediate medical attention. If the subject is able to drink and wants to do so before a medic can see them, you are still strongly advised to consult a professional over the telephone beforehand. Furthermore, do not offer headache tablets, no matter how much a subject may persist; even readily available ones, such as ibuprofen and aspirin, as these may aggravate the symptoms:

- vomiting
- extreme tiredness
- cramps
- dizziness
- convulsions (involuntary muscle contractions)
- headaches
- weakness
- muscle spasms
- confusion
- loss of consciousness

Perspiration and sodium secretion

The volume of perspiration that is lost during intense training varies significantly, from less than one litre an hour to over three litres an hour. **If an athlete perspires at an average rate of one litre an hour, this means a loss of 0.7g to 1.2g of sodium**, though some sources suggest a high-end average loss of up 3.6g. Even though not meeting the minimum sodium requirements through the diet is unlikely, it is conceivable for athletes to go below the minimum if involved in endurance training, especially in hot conditions.

The minimum sodium requirement is about 0.5g for an average healthy adult, male or female, to ensure basic physiological functionality. However, this may still be dangerously low, particularly for those in training, so a suggested **minimum of 1.5g of sodium** is often quoted. Comparing the minimum sodium intake with the recommended maximum (men 2.8g, women 2g), the threshold is clearly quite tight, but in practice people tend to go over the maximum, rather than under the minimum, unless on a special low-sodium diet. Nonetheless, if an athlete partakes in endurance training for just one hour on a hot day, and has had only one meal (say) beforehand, they could easily secrete too much sodium and other electrolytes through perspiration.

The amount of electrolyte secretion varies from person to person, and the data we have normally comes from very small group trials of athletes, since testing non-athletes is difficult and often risky. Nonetheless, the available data does not normally deviate too much from that below, but it should be considered as nothing more than a rough guide:

- sodium loss: 0.9g a litre
- chlorine loss: 1.35g a litre
- potassium loss: 0.2g a litre
- calcium loss: 0.015g a litre
- magnesium loss: 0.0013g a litre

The main concern is sodium and chlorine loss; the other electrolyte losses are so small that an imbalance is unusual, and far more likely to come from a poor diet rather than through perspiration. Interestingly, although acclimatisation and increased levels of fitness mean the athlete perspires *more*, it normally results in the athlete secreting *less* sodium.

Salt tablets

These are rarely, if ever, a good idea for sportspeople, regardless of training intensity, level of heat and humidity, or any other factor. At worst they contain high amounts of sodium chloride that produce concentrated levels of sodium in the stomach. This means that the body has to use extra fluid to dilute it, causing a delay in rehydration and stomach emptying; clearly, this defeats the objective. At best they might also contain potassium (and other minerals), the combined benefits of which have already been mentioned, but this seems rather pointless since all of this and more can be achieved from one source; an isotonic or a hypotonic sport drink *(see later)*, which will also include the required carbohydrates and fluid. That apart, the suggested doses on salt tablet packets is often five to ten tablets a day; with a typical sodium content of about 0.2g a tablet, this works out to be a large daily intake of between 0.9g and 1.8g of sodium.

Apart from athletes, salt tablets are also often recommended to those who spend a long time on the beach or to those who work in hot and humid environments, such as kitchens, factories and warehouses. However, the advice is still the same: a sports drink is still much safer and much better, whereas salt tablets are potentially dangerous and a needless expense.

As a condiment, **sea salt** is sometimes suggested as a more wholesome option as it is unrefined and contains about two per cent of other minerals. Certain sea salts, such as Solo (from Iceland), contain about 60 per cent less sodium than table salt, and Himalayan Crystal Salt boasts some 84 minerals. However, whilst these are indeed better options at meal times than table salt (and may be kinder to the palate), they should never be part of your training intake apart from what you may have used in a homemade sport fluid *(see 6.7)*. Salt tablets should only be taken if administered by a doctor; for sports people this is probably only going to happen as part of the treatment for hyponatraemia.

6.5 Sport fluids

In general, the role of sports drinks is to replenish fluid, energy and electrolytes that have been depleted from exercise. Some sports nutrition sites separate them into two main types, fluid replacement drinks and energy replacement drinks. However, this is misleading because sports drinks always provide both fluid and energy to a greater or lesser degree. There are three main types available commercially: hypotonic, isotonic and hypertonic, although all of these are easily made at home *(see 6.7, **Homemade sport fluids**)*.

Hypotonic fluid

Hypotonic drinks are more diluted than isotonic and hypertonic ones, providing less than 4g of carbohydrates per 100ml of fluid (so, strictly speaking this includes plain water), and they are absorbed faster than just plain water since they contain fewer dissolved particles than blood plasma. They are recommended for athletes who participate in activities that do not need (or use) a great deal of muscle sugar, such as horse racing, gymnastics, tennis and aerobics; for these sports, fluid replacement is more important than glycogen replacement, so hypotonic fluid is suitable before, during and after the activity. However, hypotonic drinks are generally better as a post-training fluid, or during a break between events or for sports in general.

If you are using low-fat milk as a post-training fluid there is no need to add protein or carbohydrates, as there is already ample of each; in fact, low-fat milk contains about 5g of carbohydrates per 100ml of fluid, which makes it an isotonic drink. However, you may need to add some electrolytes as the content is quite low.

Isotonic fluid

Isotonic drinks contain about the same number of particles of dissolved substances (including carbohydrates) as blood plasma, and are thus absorbed at least as fast as plain water. Those sold commercially contain 4-8g carbohydrates per 100ml of fluid. Theoretically speaking, isotonic drinks give the perfect balance between replacing lost fluid and providing fuel.

Hypertonic fluid

Hypertonic drinks contain over 8g of carbohydrates per 100ml of fluid - pure orange juice, for example (just over 10g of carbohydrates per 100ml) - and since they generally contain more dissolved particles than blood plasma they are absorbed more slowly than plain water. Hypertonic drinks are normally used post-exercise to top up muscle glycogen stores, though it is far easier to treat glycogen replenishment separately using gels or other non-fluid forms.

In most cases they are not suitable during exercise since they take a long time to empty from the stomach, and can therefore cause stomach cramps and other upsets. Some make an exception for high-endurance events when an easy form of high energy is required throughout the event, but in such cases isotonic drinks will also be required to provide faster fluid replacement. It seems that an unnecessary confusion can arise between fluid and glucose intakes, so in such cases it is (once again) better to ingest carbohydrates separately using gels or other easily ingested non-fluid forms. No matter, for the sake of completion, a homemade solution has been, reluctantly, provided *(see 6.7.4)*.

Glycerol (also glycerine)

Glycerol is a type of carbohydrate found in several foods and beverages, which has a similar calorific value to table sugar, yet it does not raise blood sugar. Adding glycerol to fluids eases hyper-hydration whilst also guarding against dehydration, and can increase body water by over one litre without causing diuresis or discomfort. This property of glycerol was first documented in the late 1980s, but it was only in recent years that it has gained the trust of sport scientists in general. However, the best timings and proportions by using glycerol are still far from being standardised, so it is important to note that (for simplicity) those suggested in this text are taken from just one paper published in 2010.

The side-effects from glycerol usage include nausea, gastrointestinal discomfort and light-headedness, but these are rare occurrences. Some people have a naturally low tolerance to certain substances, but that apart, a likely cause of side effects is from solutions that contain too much glycerol. This often happens when sports fluids are homemade, especially by the inexperienced. In recent times, some sports drinks have started to include glycerol, but they may not be tailored to your specific needs so check the amount carefully. However, even if a commercial sports drink has too little glycerol to meet your specific needs, you should still get some hydration benefits.

6.6 Fluid cycle

The fluid cycle refers to the entire hydration process before, during and after exercise. It is perhaps the most important part of this book and probably among the more challenging, so it is advisable to read it carefully and at least twice. Understanding the principles is more important than following each calculation meticulously since individual calculations can be easily obtained from the accompanying Excel program.

6.6.1 Pre-training fluid

The idea of pre-training hydration is to enhance thermoregulation and also to increase blood plasma volume to maintain cardiac output. The recommended intake of pre-training fluid is often suggested at 400-600ml about two hours prior to training, but this is perhaps too generalised, even if assuming temperate conditions. Moreover, some sources further suggest that you can drink as much you find comfortable; yet some people can comfortably drink large amounts of water. So, if the two-hour time gap before training is observed, an excessive initial intake may cause **dieresis** (increased or excessive production of urine) before exercise begins; thus rendering the pre-training fluid useless. A more sensible guide for temperate conditions is to drink according to your body mass:

- about 5-7ml of fluid per kg of body mass in temperate conditions

Example

Assume an athlete has a body mass of 70kg. Multiplying 70 by 5 and then 7 gives 350 and 490, respectively. So this athlete should consume between 350ml and 490ml of fluid about two hours before training.

Certain conditions may well demand considerably more fluid, but some people simply require more regardless of the conditions; many individuals need as much as 10ml of fluid per kg of body mass. Moreover, the fluid intake time gap before training varies considerably from person to person; many only need 30 minutes before training, whilst others need two hours or more. The only sure way is to experiment with both the time gap before training and the corresponding fluid intake volume, but you must ensure this information is known well in advance of any event. It is also worth noting that such time gaps and fluid intake volumes will change, perhaps because of age, increased fitness levels or the event itself; whatever the reason, it is worth reviewing every so often and certainly if you feel the need.

At the pre-training stage, being slightly under-hydrated, or slightly over-hydrated, is unlikely to cause any serious health problems; though it may hinder performance somewhat. Drinking too close to your training time, or too much, may cause an unwelcome interruption in your event; drinking too little may cause early dehydration.

As already mentioned, drinking copious amounts of fluid before an event is generally inadvisable, yet it is sometimes necessary to hyper-hydrate, such as before long endurance events, especially those in hot-humid conditions. The main problem is diuresis, but there is a way round this; the addition of glycerol to your fluid.

Glycerol and pre-training fluid

The main reason athletes include glycerol in their pre-training sport fluid is for its capacity to increase water retention (hydration) without diuresis. Some also believe that glycerol significantly increases endurance ability and thermoregulation, but opinions on this still vary considerably.

Calculation: glycerol for pre-training fluid (mainly endurance in hot conditions)

1. Find the value of: 1-1.2g of glycerol for each kg of body mass.
2. Find the value of 26ml of fluid for each kg of body mass.
3. The amount of glycerol obtained from *1.* should then be added to the amount of fluid obtained from *2.* Shake the solution vigorously.
4. Ingest this solution over a 60-minute period, but begin 30 minutes before you exercise; you will have to experiment to find out how much, and at what intervals, is best for you. Note that, with the addition of glycerol your first intake (30 minutes before training) may be considerably higher than usual.

NOTE: Even with the inclusion of glycerol, this is a lot of fluid to be ingested in a relatively short time (see the example below) so close to participation. It is vital that you test your toleration levels long in advance of any event by building up to the suggested intake. If you feel that the suggested amount is going to be too much regardless, then that is a good enough reason to ingest less, even half that suggested will be of benefit. As for timing, ingesting glycerol at much more than 30 minutes before training is pointless because its effects are short-lived.

Example: pre-training glycerol intake

Assume an athlete has a body mass of 70kg, then:

1. $1.0 \times 70 = 70$ and $1.2 \times 70 = 84$. So the amount of glycerol is 70-84 g.
2. $26 \times 70 = 1820$. So the amount of fluid is 1820ml.
3. Add the 70-84g of glycerol to the 1820ml of fluid and shake vigorously.
4. Begin ingestion 30 minutes before you exercise, but keep in mind that this solution should last 60 minutes. To begin with, this athlete might choose to intake 800ml or more; experimentation is the only way to find out.

As you can see, the intake advice on fluids that contain glycerol has already stepped over the pre-training period; its potential usage continues into mid-training and extends to post-training, so we shall return to it in the relevant sub-sections later in this chapter.

Carbohydrates and pre-training fluid

Even though glycerol is a type of carbohydrate, it has the special role of hyper-hydration only, so it should not be considered as part of any usual carbohydrate intake; that is the job of glucose. If you do need pre-training carbohydrates (see **2.3.1**), these will be in addition to any glycerol that you might also require.

Types of pre-training fluid

Plain water is normally fine, even if your fluid requires the addition of glycerol and/or glucose. Some sources suggest sports drinks as pre-training fluid specifically because they include electrolytes that will in turn cause you to drink more, but this not a sensible reason to do so. That apart, consuming sports drinks pre-exercise is unlikely to cause any major health problems - perhaps discomfort and underperformance at worst - but they are not cheap, so it is better to save them until they are necessary. The only time that it might be a good idea to consume a sports drink (that includes electrolytes) pre-training, is if you are already perspiring profusely. However, if this is the case, then the conditions might not be suitable for exercise or competition anyway, and if possible you should seriously consider postponing.

6.6.2 Mid-training fluid

It is whilst exercising that fluid loss potential is greatest; not only are you using up a lot of water (mainly from perspiration and respiration), but you are also likely to have fewer opportunities to rehydrate. It is perhaps the advice for hydration during training that has caused most fluid-related problems and misconceptions. Up to the late 1960s, athletes were specifically advised against drinking during exercise because it was thought that doing so would adversely affect performance. By the mid-1970s, research in this area had clearly demonstrated that fluid intake during exercise was, in fact, essential. Yet, even by the mid-1980s, the advice to drink during exercise seemed not to have filtered through to the general public, and it was often treated with suspicion even by professional trainers of various disciplines, including games teachers in schools and martial arts instructors. By the early 1990s though, the idea seemed to have gone to the opposite extreme. Drinking plenty of water was seen (and still is) on television advertisements and websites, in health leaflets and exercise centres, and professional trainers continually emphasised it; people were, and many still are, drinking excessively. It is now over 40 years since the first publication advised us to ingest fluid during exercise, but the advice is still frequently inconsistent and misinformed.

It is still commonly advised that an athlete should drink about 150-350ml fluid every 15-20 minutes during exercise; the idea is to replace all water lost through perspiration and respiration before dehydration occurs. This is often appended with more contentious advice: *don't wait until thirsty, as it is a sign that you are already dehydrated*, or: *drink as much as you comfortably can;* yet these guides could cause more problems. It does, of course, depend on the event and the conditions, but even so, if someone decided that they needed the maximum 350ml of fluid every 15 minutes, they would be ingesting 1400ml of water in an hour. This is way too much, even elite marathon runners drink no more than 800ml an hour (the recommended maximum for any athlete), and is likely to hinder performance and cause discomfort - and may also cause hyponatraemia. Trying to prevent dehydration during training by drinking large amounts is inadvisable; you should drink *ad libitum*, rather than according to set amounts that may not be suitable. In any case, a body mass reduction of less than two per cent owing to fluid loss will not significantly affect your performance or wellbeing *(see also 6.3.2)*. To exacerbate the problem of excessive drinking, the concept of perspiration rate testing to find your hourly fluid intake during training is still very much in use; it is explained next.

Perspiration rate testing

The idea of perspiration rate testing is to find out how much fluid you should ingest during each hour of training depending on the intensity and duration of the activity. It is a very simple calculation, and is still very commonly found on websites and in books dedicated to sports nutrition and sport science. However, it is *not* recommended in this text because:

- Perspiration levels are not linear - i.e. not necessarily the same from one hour to the next.
- The calculated intake is likely to conflict with the recommendation of drinking *ad libitum*.
- But most significantly, the calculation often produces an hourly fluid intake that is way too much - to the point of being harmful or even fatal.

The main point of concern is drinking excessively, so a typical method (with an example) of how to calculate perspiration rates is given below to demonstrate this issue:

Note: pre-exercise mass refers to minimum clothing and *after* urination, and post-exercise mass refers to minimum clothing, towel-dried and *before* urination.

1. Fluid deficit (kg): pre-exercise BM (kg) - post-exercise BM (kg)
2. Total fluid loss (L): fluid deficit (L) + fluid consumed during exercise (L)
3. Sweat rate = total fluid loss (L)/exercise duration (h)

Example

Assume an athlete has a pre-training BM of 59kg and a post-training BM of 58kg, and that this athlete ingested a total of 1L of fluid during an hour and a half of training.

1. Fluid deficit: 59kg - 58kg = 1kg
2. Total fluid loss: 1.0L + 1.0L = 2L
3. Sweat rate: 2L/1.5 h = 1.3L/h (1dp)

So according to the calculation, this individual should drink 1.3L of fluid an hour; **this is 500ml more than the maximum any athlete should drink during an hour of training**; if this athlete took this advice during an event that lasted several hours the outcome could be conceivably life-threatening.

Cold water concerns

Some have suggested that drinking ice-cold water, or even just cold water, is not good for athletes during or just before training. This probably comes from the misconception that cold water burns much-needed energy via dietary-induced thermogenesis (DIT); in fact, the calories burned from cold or even ice-cold water (close to freezing) is negligible *(see 5.2.2 for the details of DIT and the calories burned from cold water ingestion)*. Indeed, drinking cold fluids during or before exercise reduces heat accumulation and consequently improves endurance ability - perhaps because cold water is absorbed faster than water that is at room temperature or body temperature. Even if performance is not your main aim, cold fluid is certainly more appealing than warm water at any time during your fluid cycle, particularly in hot-humid conditions.

Cold stimulus headache

The only concern about drinking very cold water too quickly is that it may cause a cold-stimulus headache, commonly known as 'ice-cream headache' or 'brain freeze'. This can happen when very cold substances make contact with the roof of the mouth or when they are swallowed; it is the direct result of the quick cooling and re-warming of the capillaries in the sinuses. It takes about 10 seconds for the headache to start and normally peaks over 20 to 60 seconds; it seems a very short time, but as you may know, the pain can be unbearable. Apart from not ingesting fluid that is near to freezing, the easiest way to avoid cold-stimulus headaches is to drink more slowly.

Bottle tip

Before you begin training, make sure your fluid is accessible, the correct type *(see below)* and that there are adequate amounts of it - plastic bottles are safest, and those with measurements make it easier for you to see how much you are ingesting during an event or a training session. Sports caps are also advisable because they prevent you from drinking too quickly, but still remember to tip the bottle (bottom end up) first so that the water covers the lid area completely before you intake any fluid; otherwise you will take a gulp of air with the liquid and this can cause coughing and choking. Drink between breaths, and if your sport allows you to pause, do not drink immediately after stopping - get your breath first.

Glycerol usage mid-training

The addition of glycerol to your training fluid may also be useful during endurance events that last for more than two hours, particularly in hot-humid conditions, as it will delay dehydration. The method of finding the suggested intake for endurance athletes is given below:

1. Find the value of 0.125g of glycerol for each kg of body mass.
2. Find the value of 5ml of fluid for each kg of body mass.
3. The amount of glycerol *obtained* from *1.* should then be added to the amount of fluid obtained from *2.* Shake the solution vigorously. It is probably better to make a solution in lots of 1000ml *(see the note at 3. in the example below).*
4. Ingest this solution *ad libitum* - which may be mixed with other ingredients - during your training session or event. Remember, if glycerol is part of your pre-fluid intake, then this new solution should not be ingested until the pre-training glycerol solution is finished - 30 minutes into your training. If the addition of glycerol is deemed necessary for your pre-training fluid, then it should probably be included in your mid-training fluid as well if your session will last for more than two hours.

Example

Assume an athlete has a body mass of 70kg, then:

1. $0.125 \times 70 = 8.75$. So the amount of glycerol is 8.75g.
2. $5 \times 70 = 350$. So the amount of fluid is 350ml.
3. Add the 8.75g of glycerol to the 350ml of fluid and shake vigorously. **Note:** Since this is a ratio of 8.75g of glycerol to 350ml of fluid, this is the same as 1g of glycerol for every 40ml of fluid (obtained by dividing both sides of the ratio 8.75:350 by 8.75 to give 1:40). Such ratios are useful for obtaining 1000ml solutions; in this case 1000ml of fluid should contain 25g of glycerol.
4. Ingest this solution, which may be mixed with other ingredients, *ad libitum.*

Types of mid-training fluid

The type of fluid that should be ingested during exercise depends largely on the duration and the intensity, so they have been separated accordingly; for each recommendation you should assume temperate conditions unless otherwise stated. In all cases you should drink *ad libitum* of the suggested fluid, but no more than 800ml an hour. However, if your pre-training solution includes glycerol (remember, this solution will last into the first 30 minutes of your training), then the 800ml threshold may be broken within the first hour of training only; thereafter, 800ml of fluid an hour is the absolute maximum.

Low-to-moderate intensity up to 60 minutes: power walking, light jogging, shadow boxing, light bag work are all examples of low-to-moderate intensity training. Fluid losses will normally be quite small, so plain water is good enough and fast enough as a fluid replacement.

High-intensity up to 60 minutes: high-intensity exercise (such as a boxing bout) and/ or **exercise under hot-humid conditions** require fast fluid replacement to prevent dehydration - **hypotonic or isotonic drinks are preferable**.

High-intensity over 60 minutes but less than two hours: includes football, hockey and rugby matches, and events such as half-marathons, but this depends on your fitness level; if you take longer than two hours, then treat it as an endurance event. In such sports or events, the need for carbohydrates is greater than those mentioned above because you will be using more energy. So **isotonic drinks are recommended** owing to their balance of both fluid and carbohydrates; for some, the glucose level in hypotonic drinks may be too low.

Recall that if you know you will exceed one hour's training, then your carbohydrate intake needs to take place before fatigue sets in, as it takes at least 30 minutes for the carbohydrate to be absorbed into the bloodstream. You will also need to consider the other carbohydrates that you will be taking separately (perhaps in gel form) as part of the carbohydrate cycle - your total intake, including those from fluids, should be between 30g and 60g *(see 2.3.3)*.

In cold conditions we tend to perspire less and more slowly, even whilst exercising intensely. In such cases, or even for the sake of training harder, it might be worth trying glucose polymer drinks since they provide more energy yet still provide a reasonable amount of fluid. However, many athletes find that they cause stomach upsets, and that the isotonic and hypotonic drinks work just as well without any such discomfort. In addition to this potential drawback, unlike isotonic and hypotonic drinks, glucose polymer drinks cannot be homemade and thus work out very costly.

Endurance events: includes anything of long distance, such as full marathons, triathlons, long-distance cycling, hiking and climbing. For these, or similar, events, it is best to ingest an **isotonic sports drink**, but no more than 800ml of fluid an hour (the inclusion of glycerol may cause you to exceed this in the first hour, though). Once again, you will also need to consider your carbohydrate intake from the carbohydrate cycle.

Elite endurance athletes normally ingest between 200ml and 800ml of fluid an hour, whereas the slower runners may ingest about 400ml to 800ml, whilst both drinking *ad libitum*. The slowest runners are more at risk from hyponatraemia as they have more time to drink, and they are often unnecessarily encouraged to drink as much as is tolerable; such athletes do not accumulate a lot of body heat and therefore lose comparatively little fluid, and to make matters worse, excessive fluid ingestion is all too easy because of their slow pace. Those that take four or more hours to complete a full marathon are most at risk; drinking over 800ml an hour could be fatal.

Events over 60 minutes in hot-humid conditions: includes any event or exercise in hot-humid conditions that exceeds a continuous 60 minutes, or even a total of 60 minutes. So this includes events in hot-humid conditions, such as football matches with two 45-minute halves or boxing bouts with the potential to last an hour or more. As for endurance events, **isotonic sport drinks** are best (maximum 800ml an hour), and you will also need to consider your carbohydrate intake from the carbohydrate cycle.

Ultra-endurance events: advice for such events, regardless of conditions, should come only from the personal and professional guidance of well-qualified sport physicians.

6.6.3 Post-training fluid

A simple method is to drink **120 to 150 per cent of the amount of fluid that you lost during training**, over a two-to-four hour period. To calculate your post-training fluid amount you first need to find your fluid loss:

Calculating fluid loss

Pre-exercise body mass should be calculated in minimum clothing and *after* urination; post-exercise body mass should be taken with minimum clothing, towel-dried and *before* urination.

1. Note your pre-exercise body mass.
2. Note your post-exercise body mass.
3. Find your fluid deficit: subtract **2.** from **1.** - *not* the other way round.
4. Multiply the result from **3.** by 1.2 and 1.5 to obtain the lower and upper amounts, respectively, of fluid that you need to replenish.

Example

Assume an athlete has a pre-training body mass of 62kg and a post-training body mass of 60.8kg, then following the steps above gives:

1. Pre-exercise body mass: 62kg
2. Post-exercise body mass: 60.8kg
3. Fluid deficit: **1.** - **2.** = 62kg - 60.8kg = 1.2kg
4. 1.2kg × 1.2 = 1.44kg; 1.5kg × 1.2 = 1.8kg

So this athlete has a fluid loss of 1.2kg, which is approximately 1.2L (since 1L ≈ 1kg) or 1200ml. So, from **4.**, she needs to replace between 1440ml and 1800ml of fluid over a two-to-four hour period. Incidentally, if your fluid loss turns out to be negative, this means your post-exercise body mass was greater than your pre-exercise body mass; in which case, your mid-training fluid intake might have been excessive and should be reviewed.

Glycerol and post-training fluid

If you required the addition of glycerol in your pre-training and mid-training fluids, then you may also need to include it in your post-training fluid. The addition of glycerol in post-training fluid has shown to accelerate the restoration of blood plasma volume; this might be necessary if you need to rehydrate faster than normal - for instance, if you are competing in particularly hot and humid conditions and/or in more than one event and you have little time to rehydrate properly between them. The method of finding the suggested intake is given below:

1. Note down the value of your body mass in kg.
2. Find the amount, in litres, of post-training fluid you require (see the **Calculating fluid loss** method, above).
3. Divide the value at **2.** by 1.5
4. Multiply your result from **1.** by the result from **3.** This result gives you the amount of glycerol that you should add to your post-training fluid found at **2.**

Example: post-training glycerol intake

Assume an athlete has a normal body mass of 62kg, then:

1. The noted value is: 62
2. From the previous example this worked out to be between 1440ml and 1800ml. This athlete decides to take the average as her post-training fluid intake, which is: 1620ml or 1.62L.
3. 1.62/1.5 = 1.08.
4. The result from **1.** times the result from **3.** is: $62 \times 1.08 = 67$ (nearest whole number). So this athlete needs to mix her 1620ml of post-training fluid with 67g of glycerol.

Types of post-training fluid

Plain water may dilute the sodium content in the blood and thus increase your urine output, which in turn may cause you to stop drinking before you are fully rehydrated, so it is better to drink sport fluids. The fluid temperature seems to have no influence on diuresis, but warmer fluid is less palatable, and some athletes complain that it makes them feel nauseated.

In general, **isotonic or hypotonic sports drinks are recommended for sports that necessitate rapid fluid replenishment**, since the glucose (carbohydrate) content of up to about 8g per 100ml will promote fluid absorption. Hypertonic sports drinks, on the other hand, have more than 8g glucose per 100ml of fluid, so they will slow down the absorption rate. Nonetheless, **for power-based sports** that do not require a particularly rapid fluid replenishment (or copious amounts), **hypertonic drinks might be preferable**. In any case some, sports demand that you prioritise quick muscle glycogen refuelling over fast fluid replacement, but in such cases your glucose replenishment source should be treated as separate from your fluid replenishment.

In recent years, low-fat milk (with electrolytes added) has shown to be even better (often significantly better) than sports drinks for post-exercise rehydration. There has been enough research to recommend it here as an alternative to sports drinks - especially over commercial ones - as they work out expensive over time. The amount and ingestion period remain the same as for any other fluid. If you do decide to try milk as a post-exercise fluid, be sure to test it several times, and well in advance of any sporting event.

6.6.4 General fluid intake

General fluid intake refers to the fluid ingested that is not part of your training fluid. This intake, according to some, needs to be about 500ml of fluid for every 500 calories that you consume. Such overestimates are of particular interest to sports people, especially those in serious training. For instance, consider an athlete consuming 4000kcal a day; this would mean a massive daily intake of four litres, and remember this excludes that consumed from the fluid cycle. Yet, the minimum daily amount of fluid that we require to survive could be as little as one litre (although about one and a half litres is much safer), and this includes fluid from beverages - including caffeinated ones - and fluid from food.

The common advice that everyone should drink between two and two and a half litres of water a day (about eight to 10 glasses) - and excluding caffeinated and alcoholic beverages - is not supported by scientific research. It seems that thirst is a more reliable and safe guide for fluid requirements than a specified amount for all, just as it is during training, and that caffeinated drinks can indeed be counted towards your total daily general fluid intake. Nevertheless, the idea of eight to 10 glasses of water a day is so ingrained, even appearing on some official medical sites, that an understanding of how this might have come to be is worth a mention.

Kidneys' fluid excretion rate

Over 24 hours, the kidneys can comfortably excrete about 30-35ml fluid per kg of body mass; they should not be overworked by drinking too much, too quickly. As an example, this equates to a 50-kg person consuming between 1500ml and 1725ml and an 80-kg person consuming between 2400ml and 2800ml of general fluid a day, so this might be why we often hear that we all require about two or two and a half litres. It seems that the maximum 'comfortable' amount was deemed better, for reasons unknown.

In short, the advice of 2L to 2.5L a day for general fluid intake may not be harmful, but it simply seems unnecessary and so far an unfounded suggestion; many of those that follow this advice strictly will find themselves continually excreting excess fluid. As it is, the following is wiser and easier to follow than forcing yourself to meet a fixed and non-individualistic intake:

- check that your urine is light yellow
- drink *ad libitum*
- consume a wholesome diet
- avoid too much alcohol

6.7 Homemade sport fluids

Sports drinks are easier than ever to make at home because the necessary ingredients are easy to obtain from sports shops and can be bought in bulk; in the long run this will save a small fortune when compared with buying commercially available canned and bottled sports drinks. Moreover, this will allow you to tailor your fluids to your particular needs; but that apart, many or most ready-made sports drinks do not contain enough electrolytes, and few include glycerol.

Another homemade option is to use ingredients that are normally available in the home, such as fruit juices and sugar. However, unless you are really confident of what you are doing, it is difficult to ensure that the ingredients in juices (they are not all the same) will not conflict with your added ingredients, and sugar is not as well or quickly absorbed as pure glucose anyway. However, if you insist on using juices be sure to check the amounts of all the ingredients first because some drinks will have very high levels of certain ingredients that will make it difficult to make the correct dilution - you must have the correct ratio of ingredients for the type of sports drink that you require.

It is probably easiest to use a 1L measuring jug that indicates increments of every 100ml. All powders should be weighed rather than judged with spoons (unless they came with the ingredients), because precise measures are easier to fine-tune should you need to make adjustments. In any case, a measuring-spoon is relative to the substance being measured (the sizes will vary according to the substance), and even those that come with the ingredients may not be the required measure for you anyway; alternatively, dissolvable tablet forms are easy to use and measure, but are more expensive. All solutions should be poured into a sports bottle, stirred, shaken vigorously until mixed properly and then refrigerated if preferred; do not add ice to a fluid solution as this will affect its dilution.

6.7.1 General ingredients suggestion

Before using any of the items below, be sure to check their ingredients properly; it is generally better to buy the purest form of each - i.e. those without other ingredients added – as they will be easier to tailor to your requirements and will probably be cheaper as well. The core* items you will require are:

- glucose powder

Note: any glucose ingested counts towards your required carbohydrate intake from the carbohydrate cycle; an example is given among the ingredients for each type of sport fluid.

- glycerol powder
- electrolyte powder/tablets or table salt
- mineral or tap water

* This list includes the fundamental items only, there are many other ingredients that may also be useful additions, such as caffeine or vitamin C; these are explained in **Chapters 7** and **8**.

Types of water

The labelling of mineral water in the UK must conform to the legal definitions set out by the Natural Mineral Water, Spring Water and Bottled Drinking Water Regulations 2006. There are many such labels, so only the more common ones are given below.

- **Natural mineral water**: that which is extracted from the ground, and bottled at source without treatment - i.e. nothing may be added or extracted from it.
- **Naturally carbonated natural mineral water**: that which is *sparkling* when extracted from the ground.
- **Carbonated (or sparkling) natural mineral water**: water to which carbon dioxide is added at the bottling plant.
- **Spring water**: that which is extracted from the ground and bottled at source; however, treatment may be permitted, such as the removal of minerals if levels are too high.
- **Bottled drinking water**: that which is bottled but is neither spring water nor natural mineral water. It may come from a variety of sources, including wells and reservoirs.

There seems to be some suspicion held for tap water in the UK (and probably other countries as well), but there is no strong evidence for concern. Indeed, the mineral water that you buy may have come from exactly the same source as your tap water, and more often has a far lower mineral content. The appearance of lime scale in pipes and kettles is actually a sign of its high mineral content, especially calcium, and is not harmful. The chlorine content is well within the safety levels and is used to disinfect the water and kill bacteria.

If taste is a concern, leave it to stand before drinking, to allow the chlorine to evaporate; keep it covered and refrigerated, and change it once a day. UK tap water is among the safest in the world, and must meet the requirements of the Water Supply Regulations, 1989. The tests are rigorous and frequent, and all results are available to the public.

Athletes lose about 1000mg of electrolytes an hour, or even much more under certain conditions and in certain activities, and these need to be replaced. Yet, even though both mineral water and tap water contain sodium and other minerals, neither usually contain anything near enough to replace lost electrolytes. For instance, most mineral water from around the world contains less than 25mg of sodium a litre - even some of the higher ones have only about 100-200mg a litre, and tap water in the UK can have no more than 150mg a litre - so in most cases there is no need to consider the electrolytes already in the water when you are making up your sport fluids. However, there are always exceptions to the rule; Crazy Water No. 4 from the USA contains a massive 830mg of sodium a litre, so it is better to check the amounts of minerals just to be on the safe side.

Since 1g of sodium chloride (table salt) or sea salt is recommended for every litre of water, it is better to weigh it rather than estimate (unless you are using a tablet form); a normal teaspoon is 5g, so it is difficult to judge how much 1g would be. If you decide to use milk as a post-training fluid it is best to use low-fat milk, but you will also need to add electrolytes to it - the same amount as for water.

6.7.2 Homemade: hypotonic fluid (1000ml)

- 1000ml of water
- less than 40g of glucose* powder (i.e. 0-4g of glucose per 100ml of fluid)
- 1g table salt, sea salt or suggested serving of electrolyte powder**

* You may have to consider this as part of your necessary carbohydrate intake. For instance, the mid-training carbohydrate intake is 30-60g an hour, so if you take the maximum 4g of carbohydrates per 100ml of fluid, and you are ingesting the maximum 800ml of fluid an hour, this equates to an hourly carbohydrate intake of 32g. However, the recommended carbohydrate intake after training, especially the initial post-training intake, is timed very differently from rehydration intakes. So, although there will be some overlap, the amounts will not be significant, and a little extra glucose just after training may actually be beneficial (see *2.3.2 and 2.3.3*).

** Electrolyte powders contain varying amounts of sodium so it is perhaps best to follow the relevant serving suggestion. You will notice that many electrolyte powders have considerably less sodium compared with table salt, but they also include many other electrolytes.

Homemade: hypotonic post-training fluid + glycerol

- Find your post-training fluid and glycerol amounts from the method described above *(see **6.6.3** under **Glycerol and post-training fluid**)*. Using the example in **6.6.3**, the glycerol amount was 67g in 1620ml of fluid.
- 1g table salt (or proportional amount of electrolyte powder) for every litre of fluid. So, since we need 1620ml of fluid, the proportional amount of salt is about 1.6g.

Since this is a glycerol-hypotonic solution strictly for post-training, there is no need to add glucose or protein to it; these should be separate considerations.

6.7.3 Homemade: isotonic fluid (1000ml)

- 1000ml of water
- 40-80g of glucose powder* (i.e., 4-8g of glucose per 100ml of fluid)
- 10-20g of protein powder**(corresponding to a carbohydrate to protein ratio of 4:1, respectively)
- 1g table salt, sea salt or suggested serving of electrolyte powder

Homemade: isotonic mid-training fluid + glycerol

- Find your mid-training fluid and glycerol amounts from the method described in **6.6.2** under **Glycerol usage mid-training**. Using the example in **6.6.2**, the glycerol amount is 25g for a 1L solution.
- 1g table salt (or proportional amount of electrolyte powder)
- 40-80g of glucose powder* (i.e., 4-8g of glucose per 100ml of fluid)
- 10-20g of protein powder** (corresponding to a carbohydrate to protein ratio of 4:1, respectively)

* You should consider this as a supplement to your necessary carbohydrate intake. For instance, a maximum mid-training intake of 800ml would equate to 80g of carbohydrates if your solution was at the high-end (8g of carbohydrates per 100ml); far greater than the suggested range of 30-60g of carbohydrates an hour.

** The precise proportion of protein is not as well-established for mid-training as it is for post-training, which itself is still part of much research, but even so, its inclusion in training fluids is now widely considered as beneficial. There are several types of protein powder, and many sports people blend them depending on their needs; which is best is far from certain, see *3.1.3* to help you decide.

6.7.4 Homemade hypertonic fluid (1000ml)

- 1000ml of water
- more than 80g of glucose powder* (i.e., more than 8g of glucose per 100ml of fluid)
- more than 20g of protein powder** (corresponding to a carbohydrate to protein ratio of 4:1)
- 1g table salt, sea salt or suggested serving of electrolyte powder

(* and **) - as explained in *6.7.3*.

A glycerol solution is unnecessary since the focus here is on glucose replenishment rather than fluid.

6.8 Non-sports fluid

The term non-sports fluid refers to any non-specific sports drinks, such as juices, tea, coffee and alcohol. Even though most of these are technically hypertonic fluids, owing to their carbohydrate content, we have conveniently made the distinction by including measured amounts of electrolytes and protein powders for our hypertonic sport fluids.

Soft drinks

Ordinary, undiluted soft drinks should not be used as sports drinks, especially as hypotonic and isotonic ones, because the amount of carbohydrates per 100ml will be too high. Freshly squeezed juices are perhaps nutritionally better, but they will need to be diluted proportionally, and they will also need the addition of protein and electrolytes. Diet drinks are very low in carbohydrates (or non-existent), and therefore serve no purpose as fuel replacements without the addition of glucose or sugar. As far as fluid replacement is concerned, soft drinks may work just as well as plain water but are more expensive.

Caffeinated drinks

There are many caffeinated drinks such as tea, coffee, many sports drinks, cola, chocolate drinks and green tea. They all have varying amounts of caffeine in them, some of which are listed below:

- ground coffee: 80-90mg a cup
- coffee (instant): 40-105mg a cup
- coffee (filter): 110-150mg a cup
- coffee (Starbucks short, tall, and grande): 180mg, 260mg and 330mg, respectively
- coffee (Starbucks venti): 415mg
- coffee (Starbucks decaffeinated: short, tall and grande): 15mg, 20mg and 25mg, respectively
- coffee (decaffeinated)*: 0.3mg a cup
- commercial tea: 20-100mg a cup
- green tea: 20-30mg a cup
- hot cocoa: 10mg per 150ml
- red bull: 80mg a can
- cola and diet cola: 40-50mg a can
- some sport fluids: 80-200mg** per 500ml

* Decaffeinated refers to something from which caffeine has been removed, so there is always a little caffeine found in such items; it is not the same as caffeine-free, which has no caffeine since there was none to begin with.

** The amounts vary considerably, often less than that quoted or even far greater.

The above list is just a guide, other sources may well suggest very different amounts for the same drink, and one of the reasons for this may be that such lists often provide only typical amounts. However, even samples from the same source have been found to vary significantly. For instance, in one study, the caffeine content of Starbucks grande brewed coffee ranged from 300mg to over 550mg.

As far as training performance is concerned, caffeine does have a positive effect on performance, particularly for endurance events and those requiring speed and power - although benefits to strength are still unclear. Amounts lower than 300mg a day do not normally dehydrate the body, especially for those used to a regular caffeine intake. However, for those not used to a regular caffeine intake, or for amounts above 300mg a day, there could be a noticeable diuretic effect.

It should be noted that caffeinated drinks have different effects on different people; for instance, some can drink several cups of coffee with no unusual diuretic effect, yet diuresis may begin within minutes of just one cup of tea, and last for a couple of hours. You should know your tolerance levels for particular caffeinated fluids long before any event, but in any case there is no particular need to include the usual caffeinated drinks as part of your training fluid.

As a performance enhancement, caffeine should (if desired) be part of your sports fluid (commercial or homemade) or taken separately in tablet form. Caffeine has not been included in *6.7, Homemade sport fluids*, even though it is a viable ingredient; before deciding on whether to include it in your sport fluids it is advisable to read *Chapter 8, Sport Supplements*, as it explains caffeine in more detail.

Alcohol

Alcohol intake should be minimum or none at all during your recovery; this period could be a few hours or even several days depending on the exercise or event. Alcohol may adversely affect re-hydration and the restoring of glycogen, and may also delay the repair of soft-tissue damage; if such an injury has been incurred it is advisable to refrain from alcohol for at least 24 hours. If you decide to drink alcohol you should at least attend to your recovery nutrition beforehand - carbohydrates, protein, electro-lytes and fluid - and is generally better on non-training days. Never drink on an empty stomach either, as this will increase the absorption rate.

Alcohol should never be part of your training-fluid cycle; it **has no positive effects on performance**, only many negative ones, which include adverse effects in:

- co-ordination
- reaction time
- balance
- strength
- speed
- power
- your perception of ability

It also has **negative effects on your health** that will also hinder performance, including adverse effects on:

- body temperature regulation
- blood sugar levels
- water excretion (urine) and dehydration
- personal safety

Some advise that if you have drunk alcohol, then before you go to sleep you should **drink at least 500ml of a sports drink or water for every two to three units you consumed, yet such advice could actually cause you more harm**. However, before looking at this problem, we need to consider what a unit of alcohol means; there is no international standard.

Units of alcohol

In the UK a unit of alcohol is 10ml of ethanol (the chemical name for pure alcohol), which is equivalent to about 8g, but in Australia a unit is 12.7ml (10g). However, in both countries a standard drink is regarded as containing one unit because it is according to each country's definition; other examples are: Canada (13.6g), Germany (12g), Ireland (10g) and USA (14g). In addition to this, different countries (or sometimes other parts of the same country) have different definitions of a measurement; a pint in the UK is about 568ml, but only 470ml in the USA, a single measure of spirit is 25ml in Great Britain, but 35ml in Northern Ireland. To add to these problems, many guides that are supposed to give examples of drinks that contain one unit of alcohol are often misleading because they do not reflect the different strengths. Some examples from the UK are:

- half a pint of standard-strength beer or cider (284ml); about 3-4 per cent alcohol by volume.

  Comment: many beers, especially continental lagers, have 5 per cent or more alcohol. This will bring the number of units to nearly three if a whole pint is consumed.

- one measure (a single) of spirit (25ml); about 40 per cent alcohol by volume.

  Comment: this is exactly one unit, but many places in the UK now serve 35ml singles (as in Northern Ireland), which will bring the number of units to 1.4, so two glasses of spirit would be closer to three units.

- One glass of standard-strength wine (125ml); about 12 per cent by volume.

  Comment: this is already 1.5 units exactly, but many wines are stronger (up to 16 per cent by volume) and many pubs serve 175ml (or greater) as a standard measure. Even at the lowest 12 per cent by volume means a 175ml glass of wine is a little over two units.

So, if you are a keen sports person, but you also enjoy alcohol, it might be worth knowing how to work out the number of units of alcohol in a drink; fortunately it is quite simple.

Calculating the units of alcohol

- [Quantity of fluid in ml (Q) × Percentage of alcohol (P) over 100] ÷ by one unit measure of alcohol in ml (U) as defined by the country of concern; giving the formula: $[Q \times P/100] \div U$

Example

Assume a single measure of spirit in Northern Ireland, so Q = 35ml and U = 10, with a 40 per cent alcohol content, so P = 40/100 or 0.4; thus, we have:

$[Q \times P] \div U = [(35 \times (40/100)] \div 10 = 1.4$ units of alcohol in Northern Ireland, UK. However, if this measure were served in Australia the number of units of alcohol would be lower: $[(35 \times 40)/100] \div 12.7 = 1.1$ units (1 d.p.) because one unit is 12.7ml.

Earlier in this sub-section it was explained that some sources advise that we should drink 500ml of water or sport fluid before retiring, for every two to three units of alcohol consumed. However, even if we ignore the inaccuracy of what one unit of alcohol might be, this means that if someone drank seven pints (14 units of alcohol), they would then need to drink between 2333ml and 3500ml of water or sport fluids. This is clearly a dangerously excessive amount of fluid, especially over a short time, yet many people can and do drink even more than 14 units on one occasion. If the beer were a stronger continental type, then seven pints would equate to nearly 20 units, which, according to this erroneous advice, could mean a life-threatening 5000ml of fluid before sleep. This clearly demonstrates the problems of such loose advice; the intentions are no doubt good, but the consequences of such vague and misleading advice could be extremely serious.

Alcohol and the net fluid misconception

You may have heard that 'each unit of alcohol ingested results in about 80ml of fluid loss from the body', and because of this, many may believe that alcohol consumption necessarily causes a net fluid loss (i.e. more fluid is lost than is consumed); but this depends on the total fluid amount ingested (and how quickly), the percentage of alcohol it contains, and many other factors. For example, consuming a 284ml glass of beer with a four-per-cent alcohol volume would theoretically cause a 196-ml fluid loss; this is less than the 284ml consumed, so there is no net fluid loss. However, one glass of spirit with a 40-per-cent alcohol volume would theoretically cause a 55-ml fluid loss; this is more than the 25ml of fluid consumed, so there *is* a net fluid loss. Unfortunately, even this understanding is simplistic and cannot be relied upon to decide whether a certain amount of alcohol will cause a net fluid loss. Consider the theoretical equation for the given relationship between alcohol consumed and net fluid, which was explained above.

 Alcohol and net fluid loss

- [Quantity of fluid in ml (Q)] - [(80ml × Units (U))] = net fluids (N), or simply: Q - 80U = Nml

It is not glaringly obvious without some mathematical manipulation, but this equation effectively states that you can consume any amount of an alcoholic drink that is less than (or equal to) 12.5 per cent alcohol by volume, without it ever resulting in a net fluid loss. This is because many more things need to be considered; the functioning of the human body is not so easily explained by a simple equation, and this example is no exception. For instance, apart from the fluid loss caused by alcohol ingestion, we also need to consider the usual fluid loss (especially since people often drink very large quantities of alcohol in a relatively short time), and the fact that alcohol consumption can raise blood pressure, which in turn affects the efficiency of the kidneys; the reasons are many, but way beyond the scope of this text.

The point is, trying to calculate how much water you need to replace according to the amount of fluid consumed and its alcohol content by volume, or by the number of units consumed, is clearly inadvisable. Such results simply produce a number that does not accurately reflect an individual's required fluid replacement quantity, or an individual's net fluid status.

Replacing lost fluid caused by excessive alcohol consumption

It is true that an isotonic or hypotonic sport drink is better than just plain water, especially if it contains electrolytes, but you should drink *ad libitum* rather than a set amount per unit of alcohol; it is also worth keeping some water or sport fluids nearby for during the night or for when you wake. If you suffer with a hangover after waking, sport fluids with electrolytes are again favourable, and you should again drink *ad libitum*, but still make sure you do not overdo it.

The benchmarks for safe drinking levels vary according to the country, though some have no benchmarks. In the UK the advice is:

- **men**: no more than 3-4 units of alcohol a day
- **women**: no more than 2-3 units a day
- **note**: there should also be some drink-free days

The advice used to be 21 units and 14 units a week for men and women, respectively, but these weekly maximums (and more) were being consumed in one night, so the advice changed in 1995.

7 MICRONUTRIENTS

Each of us loses or uses a certain amount of each nutrient every day, and since neither vitamins nor minerals can be synthesised by the body we need to provide them through diet. However, if vitamin and mineral intake is low, then the stores eventually become depleted and we become entirely reliant on daily intakes, and if these are inadequate, a nutritionally deficient state will develop.

The amount of each nutrient used daily by the body, that is 'the physiological requirement', is the amount required by an individual to prevent signs of clinical deficiency. It is not the amount for optimum health, it is the absolute minimum amount required before problems begin to occur. For example, if you have anaemia caused by vitamin B_{12} deficiency, the symptoms include jaundice, an inability to feel pain, mouth-ulcers, memory loss, a sore and red tongue (glossitis) and disturbed vision. In any case, such amounts are difficult to define, and there are many nutrients for which there are no known levels that are considered a clinical deficiency.

Though extreme cases of nutritional deficiency are quite rare in developed countries, there is still plenty of room for concern among certain groups. The obvious cases are those with recognised eating disorders, such as anorexia nervosa and bulimia nervosa, but there are many less obvious ones: those with child, those on poorly planned weight-loss or vegan diets, and the many poorly nourished children and elderly people. In general, athletes should be eating more than the average person anyway, so they should be consuming the right balance of vitamins and minerals by default.

However, this is on the assumption that they are eating well-balanced and wholesome foods; yet this is often not the case. Many do not plan their diets well enough, or worse than this, some even eat a restricted calorie intake, which makes it far more difficult for them to attain the correct balance of nutrients. This is a particular problem for women athletes or those that practice aesthetic sports such as body building and synchronised swimming.

7.1 The basics

Vitamins are organic compounds that function as metabolic regulators in the body; they are classified as either water soluble or fat soluble. Vitamins cannot be manufactured in the body and therefore must be obtained through diet or supplements. **Minerals** are natural organic compounds formed through geological processes; they help the body to function properly and stay strong. Minerals cannot be manufactured in the body either, and therefore must also be obtained through diet or supplements.

A **free radical** (or oxidant) is an uncharged molecule; it includes an atom that that has a free (unpaired) electron, see the diagram below. Not all free radicals are damaging - some help to kill germs, fight bacteria and heal cuts, but they become a problem when too many are formed and cannot be controlled by the body's defence system. They are highly reactive and can very quickly produce a chain reaction of more and more free radicals, which can have serious health consequences. Although it is not fully understood how they adversely affect us, they are attributed to clogged arteries, diabetes, many cancers, ageing, post-exercise soreness and more. Many pollutants create free radicals, including smoking.

Antioxidants are molecules that can donate electrons to free radicals and consequently neutralize them by stopping the chain reaction and thus preventing cell damage. Moreover, such antioxidants are able to do this without being destroyed, damaged or becoming free radicals themselves. Many vitamins have antioxidant properties, such as vitamin A and vitamin E.

7.2 Micronutrient requirements

Everyone has different nutritional requirements; these vary according to age, gender, size, level of physical activity and individual body chemistry, so it is therefore impossible to state an intake that would be best for everyone. To find your personal requirements you would have to undergo a series of biochemical and physiological tests; these might include examination of blood, urine, hair and bone marrow samples.

In 1991 the UK Department of Health (DoH) provided four distinct figures for most of our nutrient requirements, known generically as dietary reference values (DRVs). They are given below:

- **Lower reference nutrient intake (LRNI)** is for a small number of people who have low needs; about 2.5 per cent of the population.

- **The estimated average requirement (EAR)** is an amount of nutrients needed by an average person - about 50 per cent of the population; many will need more or less.

- **Reference nutrient intake (RNI)** is an estimate of the amount of a nutrient that should cover the needs of about 97.5 per cent of the population.

- **Safe intake** is used when there is insufficient evidence to set an EAR, RNI or LRNI. This amount should be adequate for most people, but below a level that could be harmful.

The intake values are different for infants and young children, and often between males and females from the age of 11; further differences also apply during pregnancy and lactation. It should be noted that other countries have different recommendations, often significantly different, and even within the same countries there are ongoing and fierce debates over what the amounts should be - especially with regard to vitamin and mineral levels. Deficient levels seem clear in most cases, as do excessive (toxic) levels, but the gap between these is wide. For instance, the Department of Health recommends that most adults should intake 40mg of vitamin C a day, whereas many nutritionists advise a minimum of 1000mg a day; however, both sides would agree that 10mg (say) a day is much too low.

Meeting the requirements

Meeting the required levels of vitamins and minerals should not be a concern for those that eat a well-balanced diet. Indeed, taking note of such levels would be impractical and take up far more time than it would be worth. However, a 'well-balanced' diet should not be the only concern; there are many other considerations.

Tips for wholesome eating and a healthier lifestyle

The following is a list of tips that will help with general nutrition, and much of it will no doubt be familiar to you. However, such advice is typically vague so some further explanations have been added.

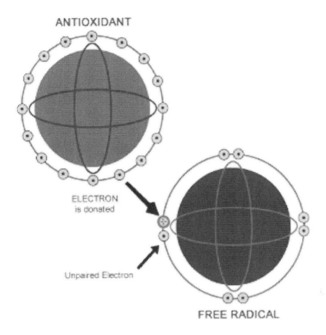

ANTIOXIDANT

ELECTRON
is donated

Unpaired Electron

FREE RADICAL

1. Base your meals on the **food pyramid** (*see 5.7*).

2. **Five-a-day fruit and vegetables**, which includes fruit and vegetable juices, is a minimum recommendation.

    a) Potatoes, although vegetables, do not count towards your five-a-day, although other root vegetables do, such as sweet potatoes, parsnips, swedes and turnips.

    b) It is sometimes unclear **how to count a portion**. For example, one apple is easily distinguished as a portion, but what about a portion of grapes? In general, simply consider a portion to be about handful or how much you can grab; as for juices, about 150ml is considered to be one portion.

    c) Juice that is labelled '**freshly squeezed**' means it has not been pasteurised, and is usually available to retailers within 24 hours of being squeezed. Most will agree that freshly squeezed juice tastes better than other types (such as concentrated juice), but it is far more expensive and does not keep for very long. Some recommend it for its nutritional content, but freshly squeezed juice is little different in this regard from other types of juice, with the exception of its vitamin C content. For example, one 225ml-glass of freshly squeezed orange may contain over 120mg of vitamin C - perhaps double or more than other types - but it is hard to say since they vary considerably. However, the vitamin C content of other types of orange juice is still considerably high, so this not a very good reason to go for the more expensive freshly squeezed juice. If you really love the taste, and you can afford it, then these are perhaps the only two reasons to insist on freshly squeezed juice.

d) **Concentrated juice** means that the natural water from the fresh juice has been evaporated - this makes the volume much smaller so it is easier and cheaper to store and package - before being frozen and shipped. Before being re-sold, water is added to the concentrated juice to bring it back to its original strength; hence the term, 'made with concentrate' or 'concentrated... juice'.

e) Juice that is not concentrated (often labelled, '**Not from concentrate**') is squeezed in the country of origin, pasteurised and then frozen before being sent for packaging.

f) When choosing your fruits or vegetables it is a good idea to aim for a **variety of colours**; it often helps to ensure that a variety of nutrients are being consumed and makes the meal appear more appetising - something not to be undervalued.

3. **Fibre** is definitely lacking in the western diet. Meeting the DoH's suggested 18-24g a day should be simple enough just by following the tips in this section *(see also **2.4.4, Fibre**)*.

4. **Eat less salt**. One easy way to do this is by not adding salt - or at least limiting it to a pinch, rather than smothering your food with it. Some find this very difficult at first, especially those who have been adding a lot of salt for a number of years, but the good news is that our tastes adjust within a few weeks, and soon the previously desired amount of salt will seem like poison. Some prefer to replace salt with a squeeze of lemon or some other low-sodium (or non-sodium) condiment or dressing. Be sure to check the amount of sodium/salt in packaged food. *(see also **6.1** and **6.4.1**)*.

5. **Smaller portions**. There is no need to pile a mountain of food on to your plate. If you are still hungry after one plate, then by all means have a second.

However, this should not be exaggerated - people often eat far beyond the feeling of being satiated; this is gluttony and leads to a very poor habit. After any meal you should not feel at all sluggish, and you should certainly not struggle to get up and leave the table or need to loosen clothing.

6. **Eat little and often**. This might be good advice for many, but it is not the case for everyone; no matter, eating little and often may be impractical. If this suits you, then it is fine, but three good meals a day with wholesome snacks as necessary is just as good. In short, do not make a big deal about eating little and often unless it happens to suit you. To insist on it would then raise the questions: 'How much is "little"?' and 'How often is "often"?' The answers to these are probably more trouble than they are worth, and by now you should have a good idea what your daily intake requirements are. So just aim to meet these without worrying too much about how many times a day you are eating.

7. **Break poor snacking habits**. Snacking can be a good way to fill the gap between main meals but it is also a very easy way to gain unwanted weight if done without caution. There is no need to demonise certain foods; if you really want something, then have it. The problem occurs when one bar of chocolate every so often becomes a habitual several bars a day, and when each replaces much-needed fruit or other wholesome foods. Snacking becomes a further problem, regardless of the snack food itself, when you continually snack for the sake of it.

8. **Be active and keep a healthy fat percentage**. A simple way to increase activity levels is to choose more active alternatives whenever possible or convenient - using stairs not lifts, walking or cycling instead of driving, and so on. Since you are reading this book you probably already have an interest in sport, but sometimes variety is lacking in sportspeople. Try some other sports or activities from time to time; perhaps you lift weights or play football regularly, so why not try swimming, climbing or tennis once in a while? It might provide a new interest, and if your regular sport is cancelled you can replace it rather than do nothing. Interactive sport/exercise video games are also a great way to enjoy exercise.

9. **Finished work does not mean finished for the day**. After work, people often get into a habit of winding down by sinking into an armchair; this can be a terrible habit, especially for those involved in sedentary work. Try to plan at

least one night a week of sport, exercise or other activity after work that does not include training at home.

10. **Don't skip breakfast**. Chose a substantial breakfast, not some air-filled cereal that is expensive, high in sugar and leaves you feeling hungry soon after. There is little or nothing better than porridge oats with a portion of dried fruit (or a piece of fruit), and it's very cheap and easy to make. People often use 'I don't have time' as an excuse; just wake 15 minutes earlier; it will be well worth the effort. If you feel that you cannot eat in the morning (perhaps the idea of food in the morning makes you feel sick), then it might be because you are still digesting last night's meal - people often eat too much and too late at night. When you wake you 'should' feel a little hungry - after all, you have not eaten for several hours so your glycogen levels are low; a good breakfast is a good start to the day.

11. **Enjoy your food**. Eating food that you do not enjoy, simply because you think is 'good for you', is not a good reason to do so, and sooner or later you will resort to old eating habits. If you are not enjoying your food you absolutely must review your eating plan - some of the tips in this section should help with this.

12. **Variety**. The food pyramid and different colours have already been mentioned (*see 1. and 2., above*), so to add further variety you might like to try dishes from different countries, or even learn to cook. Many non-western foods are easy to prepare in advance, and many can easily be made in bulk and refrigerated for use later - so in the long run you may even save time and money, and enjoy your meals more.

13. **Alcohol in moderation** is not easy to define, since we all have different limitations; so it is perhaps best not to exceed the government guidelines of the maximum number of units a week, in the UK: women (2-3 units a day), men (3-4 units a day), and both should include some alcohol-free days. (*see also 6.8, Alcohol*).

14. **Nuts and seeds** are high in protein and packed with vitamins. Although we are often warned of their particularly high fat content, they are usually high in only the important fat (monounsaturated and polyunsaturated); the less important saturated fat is usually comparatively low. Nuts (unsalted) as a snack are fine, but they are very easy to overindulge with, so be careful. Nuts

and seeds in salads, pasta and other foods are a good and easy way to add nutrients and flavour to your cookery. *(see also **4.4, Fat in food**)*.

15. **Cooking method:** In terms of retaining nutrients, steaming is generally best, followed by grilling and then boiling in limited water (you should also include the juice and keep the lid on the saucepan); in all cases, you should cook for the minimum amount of time. Moreover:

    a) Serve the food as soon as possible, and include the water (at least some) of boiled food as it will contain much of the lost nutrients.

    b) It is best to prepare vegetables immediately before cooking them as it limits their exposure to air and light, both of which destroy vitamin C - which is why the so-called fresh food from your greengrocer is not necessarily the best choice.

    c) Frozen food may lose much of its water-soluble vitamins when it is thawed, so cook from frozen, and use the minimum amount of water.

16. **Shopping:** most genuine intentions for a more wholesome diet are already doomed in the place where you do your main shopping. It is a good idea to write a shopping list before you are anywhere near the supermarket, and try not to add too many extras when you get there. Moreover:

    d) Avoid the so-called health food shops, unless it's for a particular item that you cannot get elsewhere. They are very expensive and often make exaggerated and unfounded claims.

    e) Buying the cheaper foods may not be saving as much as you think - it may even work out more expensive. For example, wholemeal bread is often only a little more expensive than white bread (and far better nutritionally), and it will keep you satiated for longer so you will use less of it. In any case, the 'own brand' foods are often less than half the price and just as good.

17. **Eat slowly**, chew your food properly and drink a little water with each main meal as required; both help with digestion, and may also help with satiety.

18. **Diet food and snacks are little or no better than what they are replacing**, though they are likely to be more costly. The sweet snacks add the further problem of bad programming - that is, they instil the idea that sweet snacks are a good option between meals.

19. **Supplements are largely unnecessary** and are often promoted by unqualified 'experts', who make unfounded claims for them. It is a highly contentious issue, so we urge you to read the 'recommended reading' for this chapter relevant to supplements before spending any money on them. Furthermore, keep an open mind when reading books written by so-called nutritionists.

20. **Fat: remove visible fat from meat**. Remove the skin from poultry, and prefer the breast (white meat) to the leg (red meat), as it contains much less saturated fat.

Food labelling

The intention was to replace the **recommended daily allowance (RDA)** with the DRVs - specifically the RNI - partly because people treated RDAs as the amounts they should aim for, when in fact they were averages rather than the amount people should consume; indeed, the RDA and the RNI are substantially more than the vast majority of individual needs. However, another reason was that the DRVs provide extra information, such as details on micronutrients, for which little information was previously available, and on fat and carbohydrate requirements. Moreover, DRVs are expressed as percentages of total energy rather than absolute intakes, and some components (such as non-starch polysaccharides) are also offered with maximum and minimum values. As it is, the European Union has continued to use RDAs for many nutrients; even in the UK, most of the vitamin and mineral levels are given as RDAs. However, many food manufacturers now include **guideline daily amounts (GDAs)** on their labelling, as well as RDAs. GDAs include more categories - such as calories, sugar, fat, saturates and salt - but unlike the RDAs, GDAs suggest a guideline of what an average person should intake. By February 2011 GDAs were featured on about 50 per cent of food and drink packs in the UK.

7.3 Vitamins

In people there are 13 vitamins, and these are divided into two main groups: fat-soluble vitamins and water-soluble vitamins. Vitamins have two names, a letter (many with subscript numbers as well) and a chemical name. The letters were used before the chemical structures were known, and are still the most common terms used by the general public. Many of the lettered or numbered vitamins do not run concurrently, and there is a variety of reasons for this. For instance, some had to be reclassified (vitamin G was reclassified as vitamin B$_2$), whilst others were later found not to be vitamins at all, such as vitamin B$_4$.

- **Fat-soluble:** there are four such **vitamins, A, D, E and K.** These can be stored in the body, so excessive amounts can be harmful.
- **Water-soluble:** eight **B vitamins** (B complex; includes vitamin H) and **vitamin C.** These cannot be stored in the body and are easily dissolved in water, so excessive amounts are excreted in the urine.

Tables 7.3.1 and *7.3.2*, below, give a list of each vitamin, including its common chemical name in brackets, the RNI values for adults (aged 19-50) if available, some of the main dietary sources and a brief explanation of its core functions.

Table 7.1 Fat-soluble vitamins

Name	UK adult daily RNI values	Main dietary sources and functions
Vitamin A is a group of inter-related substances (retinol, retinal, and retinoic acid) that can be synthesised in the body from beta-carotene (a red-orange pigment found in many plants and fruits).	700 mcg (men) 600 mcg (women) 700 mcg (pregnant) 950 mcg (lactating)	Liver (main place of vitamin A storage in animals), cheese, eggs, butter, oily fish, milk, yoghurt, dark-green leafy vegetables (spinach, broccoli, etc) and carrots. Vitamin A is essential for good eyesight and the prevention of night blindness; it is also an antioxidant.
Vitamin D	Not generally specified for adults in the UK, however: 10 mcg if pregnant or lactating, for those rarely exposed to sunlight, strict vegetarians or vegans and darker skinned people - dark skin prevents UV light from penetrating far enough for the synthesis of vitamin D	Oily fish, liver, eggs and bread. Vitamin D is essential for the uptake of calcium from food.

Vitamin E is not a single compound; it consists of eight closely related chemicals - alpha-tocopherol being the most important.	Generally, suggesting RNI values is deemed undesirable, but an average intake might be: 7mg (men) 5mg (women)	Plant oils (e.g. soya, corn and olive oil), nuts, seeds and wheatgerm (the embryos of grains of wheat). Vitamin E is a powerful antioxidant.
Vitamin K, like vitamin E, is composed of a series of related compounds.	Too few studies means that no RNI is yet suggested; however, 1mcg per kg of body mass is safe and adequate.	Green leafy vegetables, vegetable oils, cereals and dairy products. Vitamin K is essential for blood clotting; a deficiency increases the tendency to bleed or makes it difficult to stop bleeding.

Table 7.2 Water-soluble vitamins

Name	UK adult daily RNI values	Main dietary sources and functions
Vitamin B_1 (thiamine)	1.0mg (men) 0.8mg (women) 0.9mg (pregnant; last trimester only) 1.0mg (lactating)	Pork, vegetables, milk, cheese, fresh and dried fruit, eggs and wholegrain breads. Vitamin B_1 is essential for the metabolism, especially in energy production from carbohydrates.
Vitamin B_2 (riboflavin)	1.3mg (men) 1.1mg (women) 1.4mg (pregnant) 1.6mg (lactating)	Dairy products, eggs, rice, bananas and mushrooms. Vitamin B_2 is essential for the metabolism of carbohydrates and protein.

Vitamin B$_3$ (niacin)	17mg (men) 13mg (women, including pregnant) 15mg (lactating)	Beef, pork, chicken, fish, eggs and milk. Vitamin B$_3$ is essential in energy production in cells.
Vitamin B$_5$ (pantothenic acid)	None suggested, although intakes of 3-7mg are deemed adequate for men and women, even during pregnancy and lactation.	Chicken, beef, potatoes, porridge, tomato, liver, eggs, broccoli, brown rice, wholemeal bread (and other whole grains). Vitamin B$_5$ is (like B$_3$) essential in energy production in cells.
Vitamin B$_6$ (pyridoxine)	1.4mg (men) 1.2mg (women, including pregnant and lactating)	Liver, pork, chicken, turkey, cod, bread, vegetables, and nuts. Vitamin B$_6$ is essential for converting some amino acids into other amino acids, but it also helps to metabolise fat and carbohydrates.
Vitamin B$_9$ (folic acid)	200mcg (men or women) 300mcg (pregnant) 260mcg (lactating)	Broccoli, sprouts, spinach, peas, chickpeas, brown rice, oranges and bananas. Vitamin B$_9$ is essential for cell division, and also helps in the metabolism of amino acids.
Vitamin B$_{12}$ (cobalamin)	1.5mcg (men or women, including pregnant) 2.0mcg (lactating)	Liver, salmon, cod, dairy products and eggs. Vitamin B$_{12}$ is essential for the brain and nervous system, and also for cell division.

Vitamin H (biotin); also known as vitamin B$_7$.	No relevant studies, so no RNI suggested, However, 10-200mcg (men or women) are deemed safe and adequate.	Kidney, liver, eggs and peanuts. Vitamin H is essential for metabolism.
Vitamin C (ascorbic acid)	40mg (men or women) 50mg (pregnant, last trimester only) 70mg (lactating)	Peppers, broccoli, sprouts, sweet potatoes, cranberries, citrus fruits and kiwi fruit. Vitamin C is essential for the production of collagen, the absorption of iron; it is also an antioxidant.

7.4 Minerals and trace elements

Minerals, or **dietary minerals** in our case, come from the breakdown of rocks, which are then dissolved in natural water. This is why the amounts and types of minerals found in water depend on the geographical location. However, most of our dietary minerals come directly from plants that have absorbed them from soil, or indirectly from animals that have eaten mineral-rich plants.

There are many minerals required by the human body. *Table 7.3* shows most of the major mineral elements, in this case, 'major' means any for which 25g or more are present in the body, and *Table 7.4* some of the more important trace elements (minerals that occur in the body in quantities of 5g or less). Both tables provide the respective mineral's RNI values for adults (aged 19-50) whenever such information is available, some of the main dietary sources, and a brief explanation of some of their core functions. For some of the trace elements, RNI values were not set, so safe and adequate levels were provided instead.

Table 7.3 Major mineral elements

Element (symbol)	UK adult daily RNI values	Main dietary sources and functions
Calcium (Ca)	0.7g (men or women, including pregnant) 1.25g (lactating)	Milk, cheese, bread, cereal and green vegetables. Calcium is a major component of bones and teeth, and is necessary for many enzymes, including blood clotting and muscle contraction.
Chlorine (Cl)	1.6g (men or women)	Salt (sodium chloride). Chlorine helps regulate the balance of acid and alkali in the body.
Magnesium (Mg)	300mg (men) 270mg (women, including pregnant) 330mg (lactating)	Milk, bread, cereal and vegetables (including potatoes). Magnesium has many metabolic roles in the body, including energy production.
Phosphorus (P)	1.0g (men) 0.8g (women)	Milk, cheese, bread, cereals, meat and nuts. Phosphorus is present in bones and teeth and is essential for DNA and ATP.
Potassium (K)	3.5g (men or women)	Milk, meat, vegetables, fruit and fruit juices. Potassium is the main positive ion in the fluid inside cells and is essential for conduction of nerve impulses.

Sodium (Na)	1.6g (men or women)	Salt (sodium chloride). Sodium is the main positive ion in the fluid outside cells and is essential for conduction of nerve impulses.

Table 7.4 Trace elements (also known as minor minerals or microminerals)

Element (symbol)	UK adult daily RNI values	Main dietary sources and functions
Chromium (Cr)	No RNI is set, but safe and adequate intakes are believed to be above 25mcg (men or women).	Liver, cereal, beer and yeast. Chromium may be involved in the metabolism of glucose.
Copper (Cu)	1.2mg (men or women, including pregnant) 1.5mg (lactating)	Liver, fish and green vegetables. Copper is part of many enzymes and is necessary for haemoglobin formation.
Iodine (I)	140mcg (men, women, pregnant and lactating)	Milk and seafood. Iodine is essential for normal thyroid function.
Iron (Fe)	8.7mg (men) 14.8mg (women) Iron supplements, as advised by your doctor, are often necessary during pregnancy.	Milk, bread, and vegetables (including potatoes). Iron is an essential component of haemoglobin in red blood cells.

Manganese (Mn)	No RNI is set, but safe and adequate intakes are believed to be above 1.4mg (men or women).	Cereals, pulses and nuts. Manganese is an essential component of some enzymes.
Molybdenum (Mo)	No RNI is set, but safe and adequate intakes are believed to be between 50mcg and 400mcg (men or women)	Kidney, cereals, vegetables and fruit. Molybdenum is an essential component of some enzymes.
Selenium (Se)	75 mcg (men) 60 mcg (women, including pregnant) 75 mcg (lactating)	Cereals, meat, fish, eggs and Brazil nuts. Selenium is an essential component of some enzymes and is linked with vitamin E activity.
Zinc (Zn)	9.5mg (men) 7mg (women, including pregnant) 13mg (lactating 0-4 months) 9.5mg (lactating 4+ months)	Meat, milk, cheese and peanuts. Zinc is an essential component of many enzymes and plays an important role in the structure of protein and cell membranes.

7.5 Supplements

Since vitamins and minerals interact with one another, taking single supplements of either may cause an imbalance. Moreover, fat-soluble vitamins taken as single supplements are especially prone to overdosing, since they can be stored in the body. It is easiest, safest and cheapest to avoid supplements altogether unless they have been prescribed by a qualified doctor, sports physician or dietitian.

Natural or synthetic?

A strong point of debate, even though there is no strong evidence that natural is better, and it seems that the case against synthetic supplements is coming almost entirely from some nutritionists. The fact is, most synthetic nutrients are molecularly identical to their natural counterparts or are easily converted by the body to the natural form anyway. Furthermore, the synthetic form has less potential for contamination and is generally much cheaper. Many websites, articles and books that advocate the natural sources go out of their way to demonise the synthetic form, yet offer no references - or at least no credible ones. What they do often offer, though, is an invitation for their misinformed readers to buy their magical, natural super food (or similar name) at extraordinary prices, matched only by their extraordinary claims.

Time-released?

Time-released supplements are coated with a non-toxic resin called shellac, with the intention of slowing its dissolution. However, the coating may actually prevent the supplement from dissolving fully, causing some of (or even most of) it to pass through the digestive tract unabsorbed. Moreover, time-released supplements are certainly more expensive than their non-time-released equivalents, and it appears that there are no reliable papers that suggest their superiority over other supplement forms - which themselves raise many questions. In any case, taking non-time-released supplements with a meal will slow the absorption anyway, and you may absorb more and without the extra cost.

The time-released supplements mentioned here should not be confused with time-released prescription medication. If you are taking supplements, then it should be only as and when prescribed by a physician, dietitian or carefully chosen sport physician. Anything else might be a waste of time and money, and may even be harmful.

7.6 Micronutrients and sport

Regular and intense exercise does increase the body's needs for a number of vitamins and minerals, but most research seems to agree that vitamin and mineral supplementation is usually unnecessary if the daily intake requirements are met by consuming a balanced and varied diet. However, some endurance sports, those in very cold conditions and those at high altitudes may warrant the use of certain supplements. Nevertheless, in such cases the athlete should already be under the guidance of a sports physician; even a general practitioner or dietitian may not be suitably qualified in these cases - do not be tempted to self-prescribe, no matter what you may read in books or on the Internet.

Your need for a vitamin or mineral boost may also increase if you are travelling a lot, working long and irregular hours, sleeping and training at irregular times, or eating on the go all the time. All of these may adversely affect your necessary intake, so planning and eating a well-balanced diet requires a great effort, and in some cases prescribed supplements might be useful.

A number of studies have shown that many athletes, and in particular female athletes, are not consuming an adequate amount of vitamins and minerals. Athletes who restrict energy intake, eliminate certain food groups or those who do not consume enough wholesome food may require supplements as they are at risk of becoming deficient in one or more nutrients. However, in such cases, prescribed supplementation should be considered a short-term solution; it should not be used as an invitation to continue with an inadequate diet.

Iron-deficiency anaemia

There are many claims for several chemical elements - magnesium, zinc, boron and so on – that have a positive effect on performance, yet such claims have little or no data to support them. There is no clear evidence that vitamin and mineral supplementation will improve performance of an athlete who is already using good nutritional practices - although athletes who are deficient in certain nutrients may have an impaired performance. This is especially true of athletes who have iron-deficiency anaemia - a reduction in the number of red blood cells - because the body does not have enough iron to produce them. However, once the deficiency is corrected, the performance will return to its pre-deficient level. The main symptoms of iron-deficiency anaemia are tiredness and a noticeable lack of energy. In athletes it may be noticed in unusual fatigue and obvious underperformance. In either case a simple blood test will easily determine whether iron-deficiency anaemia is indeed the problem. If iron-deficiency anaemia is detected, you will be prescribed with iron supplements that will restore the number of your red blood cells to normal. If you do not have iron-deficiency anaemia, iron supplements will not improve your performance, but some athletes may benefit from them if the risk of iron loss is high. For instance, long-distance runners may benefit from iron supplements because the continued pounding of the feet may cause haemolysis (the rupture or destruction of red blood cells), especially if the running shoes have soft insoles. Whatever the case, if you do not have iron-deficiency anaemia but you think that you might benefit from iron supplements, you should seek the advice of a sports physician or dietitian first; do not be tempted to self-prescribe as they may be unnecessary or even harmful *(see **10.5, 'Iron deficiency anaemia'** for a more detailed look at this condition).*

Sodium phosphate

There have been some interesting results with sodium phosphate supplementation. In particular, significant improvements in oxygen intake and aerobic performance have been observed, but it is still early days.

Exercise and cell damage

Some research suggests that exercise may increase the requirements for vitamins B_2 and B_6, perhaps owing to their essential role in the metabolism of the macronutrients, and there are plenty of papers that suggest that certain antioxidants may be useful in the prevention or repair of DNA damage caused by demanding exercise. Many researchers suggest supplementation with moderate levels of antioxidants, though they seem reluctant to suggest details for their administration. However, others believe that such supplementation will hinder the body's ability to produce more antioxidants as it attempts to adapt to the demands of intense exercise.

8 Sport Supplements

If any chapter could be a book all of its own, this is it. Supplements are many, and more seem to be appearing all the time, but the enormity of research in this area is still hardly realised even when the number of combinations in which they can be arranged is considered. If there were only 15 supplements and we chose to research the effects of combinations of any two, three or four of these, this would number nearly 2000 trials without considering all the various sports, conditions, individuals, doses, timings and so on. If there were only 25 supplements and the same numbers were observed, the number of trials would exceed 15,000. The research thus far is just a tip of the iceberg, and this chapter merely scratches the surface of that tip.

Having at least some idea of what to expect from your supplementation is paramount, otherwise you will have no idea if they are working (they don't work for everyone) or if they are working enough for you to continue buying them. If anything, the expected improvements described in this chapter might be considered a little on the low side, but it is better to stay on the side of caution; if your gains are much greater then this can only be welcomed news.

Whilst it is true that many supplements seem to work better in combination, it is still worth knowing what to expect if you take them individually. Combined supplementation may be no better than single supplementation for individual athletes - and are normally more expensive - and if you have only taken them in combination you have no way of knowing this. If you want to fine-tune your supplementation then it is essential to know precisely which supplements work for you, in what measures, and how well. For these reasons, single supplements are first discussed without any regard to combinations, but some of the more researched combinations are briefly discussed later.

An ergogenic aid is a non-technical term for any device, method or comestible that is intended to enhance sports performance, stamina or recovery; though this text considers only the comestible ones - i.e. sport supplements, but will further include weight-gain/loss products. Sport supplements are usually one, or a combination, of proteins and amino acids, essential fatty acids, carbohydrates, vitamins, minerals, or herbs.

8.1 Supplements in context

Different results are found with ergogenic aids, depending on several factors about the subject, such as the physical and mental condition, age, gender and nutritional state, and not everyone will benefit from any particular supplement. Many of the supplements considered in this chapter have well-tested and favourable medicinal uses (and some of these are briefly mentioned), and other claimed benefits for health and well-being in general, but the vast majority of this chapter refers only to their use as sport supplements.

You will notice that many of the supplements discussed have their respective molecular formula written beside them in brackets. This is purely for information or for those interested in the chemical connection amongst certain supplements. Some of the more popular supplements are:

- antioxidants - these are covered in *Chapter 7*
- β-alanine (beta-alanine)
- branched-chain amino acids (BCAA) *(see also 3.1.2)*
- caffeine *(see also 6.8, Caffeinated drinks)*
- creatine *(see also 1.1.2 and 9.4)*
- ephedrine
- fat burners and appetite suppressors
- glutamine
- herbal supplements
- HMB (beta-hydroxy beta-methylbutyrate)
- meal replacements (including energy bars and gels)
- pro-hormones
- protein *(see also Chapter 3 and 5.3)*
- ubiquinone (Q10)
- zinc magnesium aspartate (ZMA)

Each of these, with the exception of antioxidants, will now be discussed in alphabetical order, as listed above.

β-alanine ($C_3H_7NO_2$)

Carnosine is a dipeptide (a molecule consisting of two amino acids), which is highly concentrated in muscle and brain tissue; β-alanine, a dispensable amino acid (**DAA**), is one of the two amino acids that constitute carnitine, the other is histidine. Supplementation with β-alanine seems to increase the amount of carnitine levels (a chemical compound that helps with fat metabolism and energy production), which would suggest an improvement in exercise capacity and time to fatigue.

Several studies have indeed shown that supplementation with β-alanine improves performance in multiple bouts of high-intensity exercise and in single bouts of more than 60 seconds. It has also shown to enhance time to exhaustion and delay fatigue, though it does not seem to improve strength or VO_2 max. In trials, common doses seemed to be 2-6.4g a day with no apparent side-effects, but the timings varied considerably. For example, some trials included doses of 800mg taken four times a day (a daily total of 3.2g), with a total of 90g over four weeks; whilst others took increasing amounts during the trial - in one case, an average of 6.4g a day, with a total of 146g over the four weeks of the study.

- β-alanine: suggested dosage of 2-6g a day

No timings have been suggested as there seems to be little or no guidance on this; however, many commercial products suggest just 2g a day taken 30 minutes before training. Amounts greater than 10mg per kg of BM (800mg for an 80-kg athlete) may cause paraesthesia (pins and needles), but further investigation to assess other potential side-effects and to determine a general dosage is deemed necessary. β-alanine can be found in many foods but is particularly high in animal sources, such as meat, fish, poultry, eggs and dairy products.

Branched-chain amino acids (BCAA)

Branched-chain amino acids (BCAA) consist of leucine ($C_6H_{13}NO_2$), isoleucine ($C_6H_{13}NO_2$ - the same as for leucine, but the chemical formulae are of course unique) and valine ($C_5H_{11}NO_2$) - three of the eight indispensable amino acids (**IAA**) - that are converted into two other amino acids, glutamine and alanine (both of which are involved in protein synthesis and energy production, among other things) and released in abundance throughout the body. BCCA constitute about a third of skeletal muscle tissue in the body and play an important role in muscle-building via protein synthesis.

Many studies suggest that BCAA improve reaction times, muscle mass, strength and body composition, reduces muscle damage (especially in anaerobic exercise) and increases resistance to fatigue. It is difficult to quantify most of these, but during trials many subjects had a reduction of body fat of one per cent, and increases in muscle mass of about 1.3 per cent. The reduction in fat did not normally mean a reduction in body mass since the muscle mass simultaneously increased - indeed, most subjects experienced an overall increase in body mass, though not by much. To put this into perspective would be difficult because muscle accounts for about 42% of the total mass of an average man and about 36% of an average woman (though figures vary). Moreover, we should need to compare the before-and-after percentages of overall body fat and muscle mass to understand how these BM increases occurred.

The suggested dosage in commercial products varies, as you might expect, but they seem to be about 5g taken two to four times a day (between 10g and 20g a day) and in the ratio of 2:1:1 for each of leucine, isoleucine and valine, respectively. However, researchers have used very different ratios. Some examples are: (leucine: isoleucine: valine) in the ratios (1.8:0.75:0.75), (2.3:1:1.2) and (3.5:2.1:1.7) ranging from 5g to over 20g in total a day. The timings have also varied considerably, such as three weeks before training and then during the training week at varying doses; the total daily dose in one ingestion 15 minutes before training; or set times before and after training and during the day.

In fairness, each research carried out may have had different aims - after all, the claims for BCAA are many; nonetheless, this makes it difficult for the athlete to know which dosage is best. However, some researchers have used doses in terms of mg per kg of body mass; one such intake was: BCAA at 300mg/kg/BM. This means that even an 80kg-athlete will be ingesting 24g of BCAA a day, and this may be fine, but as most research has used 5-20g a day, it might not be advisable to exceed this unless under the supervision of a qualified sport physician; so the suggested dosage in this text is:

- **BCAA (2:1:1): suggested dosage is 5-20g a day**

It is perhaps best to start with the lowest daily total (5g) taken in two or four equal doses (2.5g × 2 or 1.25g × 4). The timings seem far from established, but since the suggested benefits include a reduction in muscle damage and an increase in muscle mass, it might be better to take at least two doses close to either side of your training.

It seems that there are no side-effects from taking BCAA, but high doses may hinder the absorption of other amino acids. Red meat is the highest source of BCAA, but they are also found in other protein-rich foods such as poultry, eggs, milk and other dairy products.

Caffeine ($C_8H_{10}N_4O_2$)

Caffeine is a stimulant that works on the central nervous system, increasing alertness and concentration. It is absorbed by the small intestine within 45 minutes of ingestion and is then distributed throughout all the tissues of the body; it reaches peak blood concentration in about an hour. It has many beneficial effects on the body, but of particular interest to athletes is that it causes the breakdown of fat, which in turn leads to an increase in available glycerol. Caffeine as been shown to reduce fat, and improve cognitive skills and the efficiency of energy expenditure, which consequently improves endurance. It has also effected improvements in certain anaerobic activities, such as sprint performances and other short-term, high-intensity events - although, it must be said, far less research has been conducted on its effects on anaerobic exercise. In general, the many positive research results of caffeine intake for endurance activities have been concluded as *significant*, but each activity researched was different - often very different - so it is difficult to say any more than that with any confidence. As for the short-term high-intensity events, at this stage the finish times seem to improve by 0.5 to 1.5 per cent.

Commercial products recommend doses of about 200mg to 400mg a day, which (as we shall see) is on the low side when compared with the doses used in research trials. Caffeine in doses of 3mg, 6mg and 9mg (all per kg of BM) are considered by researchers to be low, moderate and high, respectively. As it is, most researchers seem to have used doses of 3-9mg per kg of BM before the event, be it endurance or short-term high-intensity; however, for some endurance activities caffeine was instead taken during the event at a reduced rate of 1-2g per kg of BM. Since both intake suggestions have had positive results, both are included here:

- **Caffeine: suggested dosage is 3-9mg/kg/BM before the event,** or
- **Caffeine: suggested dosage of 1-2mg/kg/BM during the event**

These recommendations mean that a 50-kg athlete would take between 150mg and 450mg of caffeine before an event, or 50-100mg during the event, and a 100-kg athlete would take 300-900mg before an event and 100-200mg during an event.

Most research suggests that caffeine intake should take place 60 minutes before training, which is about the time it takes for it to reach peak blood concentration, but improved performances have still been observed when taken within 15-30 minutes before. Some have suggested that athletes should refrain from caffeine prior to exercise, mostly owing to its reputation as a diuretic, and in such cases it seems that most are referring to caffeinated drinks, such as coffee and energy drinks. However, whilst this advice seems to be unfounded, it is the anhydrous forms - those without water, such as powders or tablets - that are recommended anyway; they work far better than hydrous forms (with water) and are much easier to measure. Notwithstanding, tests have consistently shown that caffeine does not act as a diuretic during exercise, increase body temperature or adversely affect performance in hot and/or humid conditions.

Low-to-moderate doses of caffeine (3-6mg/kg/BM) have shown positive results in a variety of activities, and in some cases, high doses (9mg/kg/BM) have shown to be even better; however, doses greater than this have not shown further improvement. Furthermore, doses above 9mg per kg of BM may show up in urine tests as above doping levels. The common side-effects from caffeine intake are headaches and insomnia, and levels over 1000mg may cause palpitations, though all of these vary considerably according to the individual.

If you do experience side-effects, especially headaches and palpitations, you should stop all forms of caffeine intake immediately and see a physician; if the side-effects are slight, then you might need to review your intake - start by lowering the dosage and the frequency. Regular caffeine drinkers seem to benefit less from taking caffeine supplements, but this is not a reason to take doses higher than those recommended.